An Italian submarine captured on a raiding cruise in the Mediterranean.

# SUBMARINES ATTACKING

**Adventures of
Italian Naval Forces**

by

ADMIRAL ALDO COCCHIA

WILLIAM KIMBER
LONDON

First published in English in 1956 by
WILLIAM KIMBER AND CO. LIMITED
46 Wilton Place, London, S.W.1

MADE AND PRINTED IN GREAT BRITAIN BY PURNELL AND SONS, LTD.
PAULTON (SOMERSET) AND LONDON

# CONTENTS

5

# CONTENTS

# ILLUSTRATIONS

Translated from the Italian
by
MARGARET  GWYER

PART I

OCEAN-GOING SUBMARINES

CHAPTER I

COMMERCE RAIDING

IT was the end of July 1940. One of my submarines
came into Spezia that morning from the Atlantic and
I went down as usual to greet her at the quay. When
her Captain, Buonomici, came ashore, his first words were,
of course, about his trip, which was of particular interest
as one of the first operations carried out by Italian submarines in the Atlantic. Then we went up together to
the Mess where a large meal was waiting—the kind of
meal a man needs after forty days at sea. Just as we
were going into the wardroom Buonamici made a remark
which has stuck in my mind ever since. All he said was:
"I must have some oranges"—but this casual remark
seemed to epitomise better than a more elaborate speech
the strain and privations of these long ocean cruises in
which hazardous operations had to begin and end with
a passage through the Straits of Gibraltar under the very
eyes of the enemy.

No one wants to indulge in rhetoric; and it was precisely for that reason that I began this book in a low key
with the story of the oranges. But the fact remains that

9

the adventures and achievements of the Italian Submarine Command during the war were far more considerable than is generally realised. I shall try to illustrate this later on by giving details of actual battles and operations. For the moment we can concentrate on one point, namely that Italian submarines ran the gauntlet of the Straits at least forty-four times with the loss of only one boat. Our single casualty was *Glauco* which was sunk on her home-ward voyage in 1941, and even she was not sunk in the Straits but one morning on the surface, 250 miles further west.

Since we are dealing with facts I must add something here by way of comparison. In the summer of 1941 twenty German U-boats were ordered into the Mediterranean from the Atlantic. They passed the Straits in the most favourable direction from a navigator's point of view and they had the benefit of all the advice and information that we could give them. Nevetheless they lost five boats sunk. This is not said in criticism of the German com-manders whose skill was beyond question; but it does give the measure of what was achieved by their Italian opposite numbers, who had to tackle the job as pioneers.

In the summer of 1940 the first question to be settled was whether to attempt the passage on the surface or submerged. There was much to be said either way. Below the surface one had the best chance, though hardly the certainty, of avoiding British destroyers and corvettes. On the other hand, a strong current runs through the Straits from the Atlantic to the Mediterranean and is bedevilled by the cross-currents and whirlpools which always occur where two seas meet. There was some doubt whether the electric motors of a submerged submarine would be strong enough to make head against it. From that point of view one was better off on the surface using diesels; but the operational arguments were all the other way.

This was the problem which plagued Submarine Command when, on orders from the Naval Staff, they were preparing to send our ocean-going submarines into the Atlantic. No one could say positively which was the right answer. In the end it was decided that the known danger of enemy patrols was less serious than the unknown navigational risks of currents and whirlpools. Consequently, when the first submarine went through in June 1940,[1] her orders were to make the passage on the surface by night, after covering her approach by a series of complicated manœuvres between the Spanish and African shores.

An outsider—and I count myself as one, having never set foot in the Admiralty—might well ask why no trial passage of the Straits was made before the war, since it was obvious even then that some of our larger submarines might one day have to operate in the Atlantic. I do not know the answer to that question. I can only say that the trial was *not* made, with the result that our submarines received the orders described above which left their captains no choice but to make the passage on the surface. In fact, they had to do so twice—once each way—because the Italian Atlantic Base at Bordeaux did not then exist and had not even been thought of.

The first two passages were made by *Finzi* and *Calvi*, both of the Spezia Group. They met no very striking opposition, spent a month at sea and returned to base, having run the English lines twice with success. The next to venture was *Cappellini*, then under Masi's command. She did not have such an easy time. Even at night

---

[1] Italy declared war on 11th June, 1940. (Tr.)

someone was bound to stub his toe on the British sooner or later and it happened to be *Cappellini*. She very nearly bumped into a destroyer and, since there was no time to dive, decided to fight it out on the surface. That night the Straits echoed with gunfire and the sea was furrowed by torpedoes on opposing tracks fired at close range. But, as often happens in these sharp, unexpected night actions, neither ship was seriously damaged, much less sunk. *Cappellini*, however, having received some hits, broke off the engagement and ran for Ceuta. It was the best thing she could have done for, if the action had been prolonged, she would certainly have been sunk. She remained at Ceuta for the twenty-four hours allowed by international law—or perhaps a little longer—and then slipped out by night and returned to base.

The next submarine, *Veniero*, not only got through the Straits but created a precedent. Her captain—Buonamici of the oranges—decided that all the underwater booby-traps which nature had put at the bottom of the Straits were preferable to His Britannic Majesty's destroyers on the surface. So he blandly disregarded his orders, dived off Europa Point and took the whole passage submerged. He discovered that navigation, though difficult, was by no means impossible. He came safely through to the Atlantic, spent a month commerce-raiding, and then quietly re-entered the Mediterranean by the same method. His was the first submarine in the world to make this passage submerged in war time.

So far we had had six successful trips.

It was *Malaspina's* turn next. She, too, made the passage submerged, though without knowing at the time of *Veniero's* success. But this time things were less easy. The natural booby-traps were in full operation and *Mala-*

*spina* had a pretty tough time. First she was caught in a whirlpool and made an impromptu dive at an angle of thirty degrees down to 520 feet; then she was thrown to the surface again only to go into a second dive heaven knows to what depth. And all this, you must remember, within a few hundred yards of the main British base at Gibraltar. In fact, if *Malaspina's* captain, Leoni, had not been one of the wiliest submariners in the business, she would never have seen the night sky again. But see it she did, after twenty-four hours of incredibly difficult navigation; and she saw it with Cape Spartel astern. By way of revenge for what she had suffered, she then proceeded to sink 25,000 tons of enemy shipping during a thirty-days' cruise. When she returned it was to Bordeaux where the Italian Atlantic Base had by then been set up.

I shall have more to say later of Bordeaux and the Atlantic Base. It is an interesting subject which accounts of the war have so far ignored. But now we must come back to *Malaspina*. Of the 25,000 tons of shipping which she sent to the bottom, 12,000 were represented by the tanker *British Fame*. Leoni has already told the story in his entertaining book of memoirs; but at least the outline must be given here, partly because the sinking of *British Fame* was our first major success in the Atlantic and partly because it gave rise to an episode which does honour to Italian seamen.

The tanker was sighted one morning in the half-light before dawn. *Malaspina* was on the surface, the officer of the watch and look-outs on the bridge and the captain dozing in a deck-chair below, when something loomed up close by. Alarm; a rapid dive. When Leoni came to examine the target through the periscope he saw that what the look-out had spotted was a large tanker, armed with two medium guns and zigzagging at high speed. A splendid target for a submarine. He closed in for the kill, fired his first salvo of two torpedoes at 15,000 yards and then dived again to await results. Just before firing he had seen that the tanker was wearing British colours. Now he waited, watch in hand, counting the seconds. He calculated that it would take the torpedoes ninety seconds to reach their mark and, sure enough, at ninety-four seconds exactly, *Malaspina* felt a dull shock through her hull, followed by a second slighter one. Apparently a hit. Leoni raised his periscope for another look. There was the intrepid tanker, still steady on her course, sailing along as if nothing had happened. It looked like a miss after all. This diagnosis was at once confirmed by a hail of shot round the periscope. In such cases there is only one thing to do—dive as quickly as possible and get out of the way, so as to dodge the gunfire, the search and the final bomb- or depth-charge. Later, with luck, one may be able to try again.

*Malaspina* went down to about 160 feet. Presently the hydrophone operator reported that he could hear nothing. Not a propeller was turning in the neighbourhood. The tanker must have stopped and if so . . . Up went the periscope again and there she was, still floating, still on an even keel, but this time undoubtedly stationary. The torpedoes had evidently reached their mark—the initial explosion showed that—but their effect must have been muffled for the first few minutes, perhaps by flooding. They had done enough damage to stop the ship, but not to sink her.

Leoni fired a third torpedo. It struck directly below the funnel and sent up a column of water which could be clearly seen through the periscope. But the tanker still stayed there, apparently unmoved. With three torpedoes inside her, she refused to sink or catch fire and did not even appear to be damaged. Obviously a phenomenon. *Malaspina*, still submerged, closed her sufficiently to read the name on her stern: *British Fame*. Leoni called his officers to the periscope in turn to see this extraordinary sight of a tanker motionless in the middle of the sea, with her guns aimed and her flag flying. Then at last it was seen that she was lowering a boat on the port side.

It took another two hours and two more torpedoes to sink *British Fame*. When it was over, Leoni was left with the problem of what to do with the ship's crew, who had been saved almost to a man. All Italian submariners, especially in those early months of the war, found the idea of turning a crew adrift extremely repugnant. Once they had taken to the boats they were no longer enemies, but fellow human-beings and, what is more, fellow seamen. The instinct to save life at sea, when it can be saved, is strong in all sailors; an ingrained part of their nature. And no one—no sailor of whatever nationality—can strip himself of all his humanity at once, even in war time, least of all of this part of it. For these reasons, Leoni did not find his problem an easy one.

Later in the war our submarine commanders received categorical orders to do nothing whatever for the crews of ships that they sank. But in August 1940 these orders had not yet been issued. Accordingly—and there is nothing surprising in this—Leoni took *British Fame's* boats in tow. It meant proceeding on the surface for a day and a night; but he did not drop the tow until they had reached a position off the Azores where it was certain that the British crew would be safe.

Since we are on this subject, I may as well add that these orders were only issued after the setting up of the Atlantic Base. Before that, much was left to the initiative of individual captains who were generally able to find a creditable way out of their difficulties. But after the establishment of the Bordeaux base, our part in commerce-raiding—in "unrestricted warfare" if you like— had to be fitted into the framework of what our German allies were doing; and it was then that our commanders received their sad education in the necessities of war.

However, no new orders, not even those of the German U-boat command, were wholly able to eradicate the natural humanity of Italian seamen. They always managed to give what help they could to crews who had abandoned ship. It was, of course, out of the question to take them on board. But they gave them food, water and medical stores; or towed their boats for a few hours till they were nearer land; or even, as Leoni did with the crew of *British Fame* or Todaro, whom we shall come to presently, with the crew of the *Cabalho*, took them in tow for twenty-four hours on end. And even so, no Italian submarine came back from an operation without some story of what it had cost her crew to carry out orders and abandon survivors to the mercy of the sea, to the cold and perhaps to hunger and thirst.

## *BETASOM*

So far I have given some account of our submarines passing the Straits of Gibraltar to operate against British shipping in the Atlantic and have just mentioned the new base which was afterwards set up on the right bank of the Gironde. But I may not have made it clear that these Atlantic operations were not simply a bright idea by some high-up in the Admiralty, but were the result of careful study by the Naval Staff before the war. We had always intended to operate against British shipping, if war came; and in 1940 we did so by the only means available. It meant working from our home-bases and risking the double passage of the Straits under the conditions which I have tried to describe. But there was no other way out. It was either that or give up the whole idea—a thing we were unwilling to do, not so much for reasons of prestige, as because there was no operational alternative. We had no choice but to rely on the skill of our commanders and expose them to great hazards at either end of each trip.

As soon as the Germans had occupied France and were in control of the coastline as far south as the Bay of Biscay, the situation changed. Our Naval Staff began at once to investigate the possibility of setting up a permanent base at one of the French Atlantic ports and operating part of our large submarine fleet from there.

The question was raised with the German Admiralty and the Army of Occupation, both of whom gave their cordial assent. As a result, in August 1940, an Italian base began to take shape at Bordeaux.

To begin with it was simply called the Atlantic Flotilla; but this was evidently too meagre for the brass-hats in Rome, who presently re-christened it "High Command of Italian Submarine Forces in the Atlantic". This very beautiful, sonorous title was rather long for everyday use, so it was cut down in practice to *Betasom*. You can derive that how you please—*Beta* for *Bordeaux* or *Base* and *Som* for *Som*mergibili. Anyway, that was what the base was normally called and the title has stuck ever since.

The command of *Betasom* went to Vice-Admiral Angelo Parona. In the first war he had served in submarines in the Adriatic. Between the wars, as soon as our submarine strength began to grow again, he had commanded a flotilla; and, immediately before his appointment to *Betasom,* he had been the Number Two in Submarine Command. He was a man of parts and one, above all, who knew how to get things done. No one could have been quicker or more resourceful in finding a way through the many difficulties that beset him. But he was not, perhaps, an entirely sympathetic character. He expected everyone to put as much into the job as he did himself; and he was at no pains to hide his feelings, if any of his subordinates fell below his own high standard. As a result he was apt to be impatient and the impatience was sometimes resented. On the other hand, he was never niggardly of praise; he could be relied on to take official notice of acts of courage, and he was always willing to give leave to enthusiasts and those whom he recognized as fighters. It was due to Parona's skill and drive that *Betasom* so quickly reached a state of efficiency which enabled it not only to refit submarines on their return from operations, but also to carry out the major repairs made necessary by bad weather or enemy action. He was also able to do much to improve the design and equipment of submarines for their specialised work in the Atlantic.

Spezia was the depot from which men and materials were drafted to *Betasom*; and the same base also provided the largest contingent of Atlantic submarines. Its other contribution—if I may be allowed to mention this —was its C.O., Commander Aldo Cocchia, who was appointed Chief of Staff to *Betasom*. On him fell the responsibility for collecting and transporting to Bordeaux everything that the new base was likely to need. "Everything" ran from dynamos for battery-charging to special rations; from engine-spares to optical instruments; from cigarettes to a complete wireless-station; from clothing to air-compressors; from small arms and guns to ammunition; from torpedoes to machine-tools for the workshop. From Spezia, too, went the establishment of officers, seamen and shipwrights, all of whom had to be provided with transport, rations and travel-orders. Finally, in August 1940, still from Spezia, went Admiral Parona and part of his staff.

In Bordeaux the Admiral found himself confronted by a row of empty, dirty sheds, which had previously been used as warehouses. There were no dockyard facilities and not so much as the smell of a workshop. No light or power was laid on. He held his first conference that evening in one of the deserted sheds. All his staff attended, sitting round on packing-cases. There was Lieutenant Fenu, who later ran *Betasom's* small but highly efficient armoury; Lieutenant-Commander De Moratti, the signals officer; Commander Capone, in charge of supplies; Lieutenant-Colonel Di Losa, the admin. officer; Lieutenant-Commander Giudice, the Admiral's Secretary and Flag Lieutenant; and Major Grucilla, the M.O. Only two officers were missing; Lieutenant Auconi, the Gunnery Officer, who joined later but made up for lost time; and the Chief of Staff, who was due to arrive in October in command of the submarine *Torelli*.

The plan of the future base was drawn in chalk on the floor. Storerooms here; engine-shop there; spares in that shed; generator over there; compressors arranged this way; electric wiring like that; transmitter in the other place. All orders were brisk and verbal: You take over this; you take over that. Then everyone set to work, urged on by the Admiral, who gave instructions, settled problems, bull-dozed his way through difficulties. It all had to be done under the appraising eyes of the Germans and the implied mockery of the French, who seemed to be saying: "Well, let's see how these Italians make out." But the work went on with enthusiasm, with the self-confidence and verve which produces results.

The harbour's wet-docks, separated from the river by two locks, had been turned over to us. There, alongside the quays at which the submarines would later berth, rose the workshops, the stores, the electric plant, the compressors, the armoury and the torpedo stores—all the attributes of a large submarine base. The Germans had also handed over the French transatlantic liner *De Grasse*, which was berthed along the outer quay of the dock. We found her very useful during the first few weeks and quartered ourselves on board, along with the Operations Room and the admin. offices, our own wardroom, the sickbay and the main wireless-station. She managed to accommodate everyone, from the Admiral to the submarine crews, from the dockyard hands to the stewards and mess-waiters supplied by Lloyd Triestino. As time went on and our numbers increased, we had to requisition another liner, the *Usaramo*, which lay astern of the *De Grasse*. She provided sleeping-quarters and messrooms for the many workmen who had in the meantime arrived from Italy. Even so, materials and spares tended to overflow into various sheds on the quay.

At last everything was straight, everything arranged as it should be. And then, on 8th December, 1940, our burgeoning base suffered its first air-raid. It lasted all of five hours. The *Usaramo* was sunk; a small steamer nearby was hit and went up in flames; bombs fell on the sheds, on the stores, on the dockside and on our M/T which was parked there. We were obliged to recognise that our beautiful organisation had one weakness. True, the submarines, the main target, were miraculously undamaged and the *De Grasse* had only received some conspicuous but harmless hits on her upper-works. But there was no reason to expect that we should be so lucky again. We had made the mistake of concentrating too much that was important into far too small a space. It was now clear that we should have to disperse. The first step was to find other quarters for the submarine-crews, who had every right to peace and quiet between operations. For the rest, we should simply have to give up the convenience of having everything close at hand. The submarines would have to be left as they were, since there was no other berth. But the office-staff, most of the stores, the workshops, the armoury and the ammunition-dumps would have to find another home. And with them—at

least at night, which seemed to be the time for air-raids
—would have to go all personnel not strictly necessary
for guard-duties.

The problem seemed far from easy; but in fact it was
quickly solved, thanks to the Admiral's organizing ability
and—I must add—the energetic and efficient help of our
German allies. A few telephone-calls, an exchange of
signals between *Betasom* and U-boat Command, and a
new organisation sprang to life. The crews and stores
were accommodated in hutments outside the danger-zone;
officers were billeted in villas or, if they were lucky, in
neighbouring *chateaux*; and headquarters, with its offices,
mess and wireless-station, set up in a small house not far
from the submarine berth. The re-organization was complete by January 1941, and remained in being until the
armistice.

# CHAPTER III

## U-BOATS

THE Italian submarines at Bordeaux, and *Betasom* itself, came under the operational control of the German U-boat Command. But for administration and discipline we were still responsible to the Italian headquarters, *Maricosom*, in Rome. We were thus involved in two distinct chains of command; but the fact never hampered us or gave rise to any difficulty. Rome was always careful not to give operational orders and the *B.d.U* (U-boat Command) never interfered administratively. What was important to the German Command was to have the effective control of our twenty-seven submarines. For the rest they were willing to rely on the spirit of co-operation which then united our two countries' forces. And in this they were right. No one at *Betasom* had thoughts for anything but victory; and we were all convinced that victory could only be won by working as closely as possible with the Germans.

We thus became part of the German organization and were very cordially welcomed. Naturally so, when you consider that the Italian Atlantic Flotilla exactly doubled the number of submarines available to the *Kriegsmarine* for the war against British shipping. That may seem surprising, for estimates of the size of the German submarine fleet are often rather vague and cloudy. It may be as well, therefore, to begin by setting down the facts.

23

At the outbreak of war Germany had no more than forty U-boats, of which only half were operational. The German High Command, especially on its naval side, had certainly foreseen the importance of the war on shipping; and yet submarines—the one indispensable instrument— were lacking. Was this due to a failure on the part of the Naval Staff or to a political misjudgment of the European situation? There is no certain answer; but the fact remains that in September 1939 Germany had only a few dozen submarines, mostly small and not very seaworthy. Of these she could only send out six or seven on patrol at a time and often still fewer.

One story, current at the time, shows up the situation very neatly. At the end of December 1939, only three U-boats were operating in the whole Atlantic. By an odd chance they were commanded by three brothers, all naval lieutenants—the brothers Sachs. German submariners used to say, fairly enough, that the blockade of the British Isles had become a private war on the part of the Sachs family.

Nevertheless, the German Navy had trained its submarine-crews well. They had carried out exercises in attacking convoys, organized and escorted on exactly the system that it was inferred that the British would use. These exercises, each lasting several days, evolved the wolf-pack tactics which Admiral Doenitz later used with so much success against British and American shipping.

The commentators have since had much to say about these tactics; but they have, I think, missed or underestimated one point of the greatest importance—the liberty of action which was allowed to individual commanders. Doenitz relied, not on issuing detailed orders, but on grounding his officers in certain basic principles which were to guide their actions. He believed, quite rightly, that if these were accepted, there would be no need for elaborate restrictions and directives. Each commander would know what he ought to do in any given situation and would be able to rely on his own skill and knowledge to find the answer to the hundred-and-one problems which present themselves in battle.

Even patrol-areas were not rigidly defined. Each submarine in the Atlantic was allotted a base of operations, so to speak; but this was only her starting-point. Any commander—novices included—was free to shift his position, as often and as far as he liked, in search of enemy convoys. The star-performers—Prien, Kretschmer, Lüth and others—were given open orders, which allowed them to indulge in what came to be known as a "free-hunt" without any restrictions of time or place.

The U-boats operated on the surface. Once at sea, each commander acted independently and made his own search, casting in this direction or that according to the clues he could pick up for himself or which were provided by an occasional signal. Sometimes he followed his own instinct entirely, more often the advice and suggestions of *B.d.U.* Days or even weeks might pass without result; then at last one of the U-boats would sight the enemy, a close-packed convoy of thirty or forty ships—part of England's life-line—with its anti-submarine escort, perhaps a shadowing aircraft and sometimes even a supporting force of aircraft-carriers and cruisers. As soon as a convoy was sighted, all the U-boats in the vicinity—if possible all those at sea—converged on its track. But it was essential that the original U-boat should not attack at once, lest the convoy disperse. Her task was to report the position of the convoy and keep track of its subsequent movements. The technique of shadowing was to lie back on the horizon during the day and close up at night, signalling changes of course at regular intervals. It meant sticking to the convoy like a limpet, running either awash or openly on the surface, playing catch-as-catch-can with aircraft and escort vessels. To keep up with a fast convoy the diesels had to be run flat out, so that the low-lying submarine took it green right over the bridge. But the look-outs, lashed to the rail with safety-belts, never lost sight of the ships they were following. Their position, course and speed was regularly reported; and sometimes, at the request of *B.d.U*, the shadowing U-boat would transmit homing-signals to the other submarines in the area.

This repeated signalling ended inevitably in revealing the U-boat's presence. The enemy would then take every possible evasive action, laying down smoke and making sudden changes of course, and would counter-attack with destroyers, corvettes and aircraft. Each gambit produced its reply, each move by the convoy a counter-move by the U-boat, so that the two duellists were locked in a tense struggle, marked by sudden turns, rapid dives, gunfire, torpedoes and patterns of depth-charges.

Meanwhile, as soon as the first sighting-report had been received, the *B.d.U* had called up all the other submarines at sea. The position of each was known at headquarters and it was decided there which boat could—and there-fore should—join the fight, even if it meant a forty-eight hours' chase. It was also decided which U-boat was the nearest to the scene of action and could join the shadower at once, help her to keep track of the convoy and replace her, if she became a casualty.

The order to start the attack proper always came direct from headquarters and was given as soon as Doenitz was satisfied that enough U-boats were in touch with the convoy to destroy it. The attack was made on the surface at night. As soon as darkness fell, the wolves ran in among the flock—the convoy which could neither shake them off nor destroy them—and the battle began. One blow followed another, delivered at a range at which it was impossible to miss, between opponents who could barely see each other. The U-boats, still on the surface, came down the lanes between the ships, each picking her own target and staying alongside until it had been destroyed by torpedoes or gunfire. Ships sank, ships took fire. All of them fought, for they were all armed, and the escorts fought the hardest. They threw themselves on the submarines wherever they could find them, hit some and forced others to dive. But once the wolves were among the sheep, the dogs could do little to bring them to bay.[1] The convoy dispersed and the faster ships tried to make a get-away. But the U-boats still clung on, following and keeping up the attack. The escorts were generally left alone, unless there was an exceptionally favourable opportunity, for the submarines' real business was to destroy the convoy, to wipe out merchant-tonnage. These battles lasted the whole night and into the following day, or even for two or three days, if necessary. All the time fresh U-boats were joining in, brought to the scene by wireless messages from sinking ships or by signals from the original pack reporting their successes.

And so the running-fight went on. . . .

[1] I am speaking, of course, of the period 1940–41; later the allies developed a defence which was largely effective against U-boat attack.

CHAPTER IV

## SHIFT TO THE ATLANTIC

A T the end of 1939 only a handful of U-boats were
ready for Atlantic operations. By the summer of
1940 there were not many more, for the building
programme was still in its early stages and may not even
have been finally settled. The Italian reinforcement was
therefore very welcome. It gave a new impetus to the
campaign against British shipping, which then seemed
the only means, short of an invasion of England, by
which the war could finally be won. Accordingly, our
main submarine fleet was transferred to *Betasom* to
operate side by side with the German U-boats.

*Malaspina*, after her first Atlantic patrol, had already
homed on *Betasom* instead of returning to Italy. She
was presently followed by twenty-six other boats—four
from Taranto, eight from Naples and fifteen from Spezia.
These included three—*Calvi, Finzi* and *Veniero*—which
had each completed one Atlantic mission in June and
July and returned to base in Italy. To the six passages of
the Straits already mentioned, we must therefore add
another twenty-seven, making thirty-three in all. We
shall come to others later. During August and September
our submarines went through at the rate of one a night.
Some made the passage submerged, some on the surface.
Some got through without incident and even without
noticing the adverse current at Gibraltar or the whirl-

pools off Tarifa. Others were less fortunate and involved themselves in tricky feats of navigation or a battle of wits with enemy destroyers. But they all reached the Atlantic —including *Calvi,* who had much the same difficulty as *Malaspina,* and *Bianchi* and *Brin,* who ran into trouble one after the other.

*Bianchi* (Lieutenant-Commander Giovannini) had already done one tour of duty in the approaches to the Straits, where she had torpedoed and sunk an enemy patrol-ship. Now she came back to the same waters, armed with a certain amount of experience. She took the passage submerged, but went off course either because she was being hunted or because she was caught in the Tarifa current, and ended by hitting the sea-bed somewhere off Point Malabata. She reported serious damage to the pressure hull, which prevented her from diving again, but was able to make Tangier on the surface. This was an international port and therefore free for all—even Italians.

*Brin* (Lieutenant Longanesi) had a similar misfortune, or one with the same results. While submerged she damaged both her gyro and her magnetic compass. Longanesi tried to make do with a small, uncompensated boat's compass, but the navigation was too tricky for such rough and ready methods. The end came when *Brin* ran ashore off Malabata Point and damaged her hull. Longanesi, unable either to continue his patrol or to return to base, also made for Tangier, where two Italian submarines were thus unwilling guests.

The British, of course, put destroyers on guard outside the harbour and set their local network of agents to work. Our people, on the other hand, carried out repairs with spare parts sent from Italy and, after three weeks'

work, were ready for what proved a brilliant and successful manœuvre.

It was a calm and splendid night at the full moon. The
two commanders were up at the club, ostensibly flirting
or playing bridge; the crews were dozing in their bunks;
and on the quayside Spanish guards were sleepily keeping
watch. Everything seemed quiet and still. Suddenly, at
a prearranged time, the two commanders reappeared on
board; the crews sprang to action stations as if by magic;
*Bianchi* and *Brin* slipped their cables and were off. Travelling on the surface, both diesels full out, they ran the
gauntlet of the waiting destroyers and got clear away
beyond Cape Spartel, leaving behind them a baffled network of British agents.

Off the mouth of the Gironde, *Brin* found a British submarine lying in wait and was greeted by gunfire almost,
so to speak, on her own doorstep. She returned the greet-
ing cordially. A heavy fog was then lying on the sea,
which gave this little battle a fantastic, unreal quality.
The result was love all, or perhaps one should say, advantage to Longanesi, since he succeeded in doing what he
wanted, which was to enter the Gironde. The English
had only the satisfaction of a little gun-play.

Among the submarines to reach Bordeaux in the summer of 1940 was *Torelli*; and the following extract from
her Captain's log gives a clear picture of what the passage
through the Straits was like:

"We dived at dawn on 7th September within sight of
Alboran Island and remained that day on the bottom,
so as to make certain of our point of departure. At night-
fall we surfaced and set a course for the lighthouse on
Carnero Point, running on the surface under one diesel.
Speed, about 10 knots; no moon; sea calm; light westerly

A tanker in the Atlantic hit by a torpedo fired from the submarine *Tazzoli*.

A tanker under fire from an Italian submarine in the Atlantic.

Scene on board an Italian submarine.

An Italian submarine arrives in the dock at Bordeaux.

breezes. At 0200 hours on 8th Sept. we dived, being then two miles south of the Rock. No ships were sighted while we were on the surface; and there was no hydrophone effect when we reached our planned depth of 290 ft., which we expected to hold for the whole passage.

"Making allowances for adverse currents, we had estimated about 18 hours for the passage. In fact, it took nearly 22; but on the whole there was little trouble. No enemy ship was sighted. Once or twice the hydrophones picked up the beat of a nearby propeller. On one occasion it seemed as if we were being hunted, for we could hear the noise of an engine stopping and starting, always very close. The buzz went round and there were a few signs of nervousness among the crew. But no depth-charges followed, nor did we pick up the characteristic high note of the enemy's Asdic. It was probably only a Spanish boat, intent on her own business.

"Navigation, on the other, especially in the strong contrary currents, gave us some trouble, though nothing serious. We were able to keep steerage way at about four knots and hold our depth within 30 ft. We experienced none of those violent leaps of 120 or 150 ft., of which *Calvi*, *Malaspina* and others had complained. It had been suggested that we should cut out the auxiliary motors, partly to economise amps, but mainly to reduce detectable noise. But, finding the boat difficult to handle with unassisted steering, we ended by keeping everything going. And in any case, anyone hunting a submerged submarine would be more likely to use apparatus of the Asdic type, which cannot be cheated by silencing machinery.

"Shortly after our first dive the echo-sounder showed a progressively diminishing reading, although in that part of the Straits the soundings should have been constant. Evidently we had lost the main channel; but it was difficult to know whether the strong lateral current, reported by almost all submarines, was carrying us north or south. Although considerable drift was apparent aften ten minutes or so, it was another half-hour before the soundings confirmed that the set was southerly. We were obliged to change course, making allowance for the estimated strength of the current. Apart from some disturbed motion and sudden variations of trim, nothing further abnormal happened until about noon. Then our difficulties began, when by dead-reckoning Tarifa was abeam. This was an area where everyone picked up trouble. In our case, we found that we were barely making headway.

"This was a point at which the sea-bed should have shelved steeply upwards. Instead, soundings remained constant or even increased. Steering and trimming were both very difficult and there were moments when we seemed about to lose control altogether. This was the crisis—a crisis which lasted in all for four hours.

"We were all in the control-room. The skipper was on his stool with his eyes going from the depth-gauge to the chart; Number One was squatting beside him. The Chief was at the fruit-machine,[1] which plotted the soundings read off by the P/O Telegraphist. The pilot watched compass and rudder and gave warning when we were off course, as happened fairly often. It was pretty cold and we were all wearing heavy sweaters. Number One had thrown a blanket over his shoulders as well, so that we looked like a group of gypsies round a camp-fire.

"To save amps lighting had been reduced to a minimum. There was one dim bulb over the depth-gauge

---

[1] The calculating-machine; its Italian nickname *pianoforte*.

and another in the middle of the control-room. In that twilight everyone looked gaunt and hollow-eyed and the general effect was that of a surrealist picture. Condensation dripped from the plating of the hull. The water-tight doors were closed. The rest of the crew were ostensibly resting on their bunks; but certainly no one slept. They were all intent on what was happening, ready to leap to their feet as soon as the emergency came, for which all hands would be needed.

"The deep silence was only broken by the telegraphist reading off the soundings, by the pilot's low voice or by occasional orders from the Skipper. Periodically the E.A.[1] would appear with specific-gravity readings from the batteries and, after conferring with the Chief, would report how we were doing for amps.

"It soon became clear that, by keeping a course through the middle of the Straits, we were making far too little progress. We therefore decided to bear up under the Moroccan coast, partly in the hope of picking up a favourable current and partly because the more even distribution of soundings suggested that navigation would be easier. We altered course 30 degrees to the south and then turned west again as soon as the soundings showed that we had 150 ft. of water beneath us.

"The critical phase lasted, as I said, for about four hours. After that there was a sharp improvement. As soon as we came in under the coast, we found a favourable current which carried us out through the Straits. It became easier to hold our course and, in short, from then on everything ran smoothly.

"At 1800 hours we refreshed the air, but more for the sake of testing the apparatus than from any real need.

[1] Electrical Artificer.

Two hours later we had a meal. Finally, at 2300 hours, reckoning that we were now far enough out, we made a careful check all round with the hydrophones and surfaced. We came up with the diesels already clutched in and a salvo of torpedoes ready to fire, if any destroyers were in sight. I was the first on the bridge. We had surfaced near a cluster of boats' fishing lights, with Cape Spartel bearing seven or eight miles to the east. Over the inter-com I told the crew that we had passed the Straits. An answering voice came from below: *'Viva l'Italia!'*"

As we have seen, a total of twenty-seven submarines got through into the Atlantic. Each of them remained about a month on patrol, operating against shipping in the area of the Azores. This was a good billet, partly because weather conditions were generally favourable and partly because most of the enemy merchant ships in that part of the Atlantic, though armed, were sailing independently. It was thus an excellent training ground for submarine crews with no previous experience of the intricacies of commerce-raiding. I don't know, for example, whether any Italian submarine commander had carried out a peacetime exercise in attacking convoys by night on the surface—the accepted tactic during the war. I don't know; but I doubt it. Nor do I believe that more than three or four commanders had ever taken a submarine into the Atlantic. It fitted in very well, therefore, that they should gain a little experience in a quiet area before facing bad weather and the British in the Western Atlantic.

It was for these reasons that we picked on the Azores; and this area became the scene of our first successes in a campaign which turned out, on the whole, not too badly. Between them, the thirty-two Italian submarines engaged sank about one million tons of enemy shipping. On her first patrol *Malaspina* sank the *British Fame* and two other ships; *Cappellini* sank the *Cabalho*, of which more later; Polizzi's *Nani* sank two ships and Petroni's *Veniero* and Bertarelli's *Baracca* one each. To these should probably be added others which I do not remember. *Mocenigo* (Lt.-Commander Agostini) hooked an entire convoy, played it with great skill, reported its position and herself sank two ships.

These results could fairly be called satisfactory—more than that, if you consider the crews' lack of training and the fact that our submarines were neither well designed nor well equipped for the work they had to do. The first requirement which was generally lacking was a high surface speed, in order to shadow effectively. The second was a low silhouette to make the submarine difficult to spot on the surface. Unfortunately, Italian submarines were equipped with conning-towers of truly prodigious size, which provided space for galleys, lavatories and what have you. It would also have been a help if there had been less superstructure altogether, whereas the bridge was in fact dominated by the massive housings of the two periscopes, to which were attached the W/T aerials and a short mast.

If you ask the reason for this unrealistic design, I can only say that very few people in Italy expected before the war that our submarines would do most of their fighting on the surface—at any rate in the early days and in the Atlantic—and would only submerge occasionally. Hence the unnecessary superstructure, the low surface-speed and the unsatisfactory hull-design.

These faults soon came to light at *Betasom*; and alterations were put in hand with that base's usual promptness. Under the direction of Fenu, our engineer, radical changes in hull-design were made and pushed through at record speed, despite our limited resources, the shortage of skilled hands and the interruption of air-raids and air-raid warnings. In this work the staff at *Betasom* had, of course, the full collaboration of the various submarine commanders; and we were in fact largely guided by their reports, observations and requests.

It fell to one of the first submarines remodelled at *Betasom* to achieve one of our most striking successes in the Atlantic. Giovannini's *Bianchi*—the same *Bianchi* that had so much trouble in the Straits—was completely refitted and re-designed at Bordeaux. She then set out for her billet, where she received a signal ordering her to attack a convoy which a German U-boat was then shadowing. Closing at full speed, Giovannini found the convoy early on the second night, when the German wolf-pack attack had already begun. He squeezed himself into the battle, sank two ships straight away and gave chase to a third. When he got within range and was about to fire his torpedoes, he found that a U-boat was also closing in for the kill. A kind of race then started between the two submarines, different from a race in a regatta only in that the prize was the sinking of a ship. It was an incident of which German propaganda later made much, all the more so because Giovannini was a well-known figure at pre-war Kiel regattas, where he had often taken a first for the Navy.

The end of the story was that both submarines fired at once and both hit. The unfortunate ship sank immediately, followed by another which *Bianchi* caught in the same chase. As soon as the destruction of the convoy was complete, Giovannini headed happily homewards, most of his torpedoes fired and his fuel almost exhausted. On the way back he had another success, his fifth victim, and arrived at Bordeaux with 30,000 tons of enemy shipping to his credit. For a long time, until Fecia de Cossato appeared on the scene, this stood as a record for a single patrol.

After this success Giovannini was transferred to Gotenhafen, where he founded a school for Italian submariners, and *Bianchi* was taken over by Franco Tosoni Pittoni, of whom we shall have more to say presently.

## Chapter V

## SALVATORE TODARO, THE KNIGHT ERRANT

I FIRST met Salvatore Todaro when he brought *Cappellini* into Bordeaux and, in the Admiral's absence, made his report to me on his first (and notable) Atlantic patrol. Though I had never seen him before, our brief interview was enough to show me his quality. Later, as I came to know him better, my admiration for him developed into a deep affection. He was a good deal my junior both in years and service; but he was naturally mature and had a strength and nobility of character, which would have made anyone proud to claim his friendship.

He was a stockily built man of medium height, olive-skinned, with a pair of keen, thoughtful black eyes, which exactly matched his short curly beard. Before the war he had been, among other things, an observer on flying duties and had suffered internal injuries in a crash, which, though there was nothing to show outwardly, gave him a good deal of pain. This forced him to go slow for a while; but in June 1940, when it was clear that Italy would come into the war, he volunteered at once for active service. In fact, he made repeated applications for a submarine command in the Atlantic—about the most exhausting job that you can imagine. The Admiralty, knowing something about his physical condition, put him off for several weeks; but in the end the exigencies of war and the shortage of submarine commanders prevailed, and Todaro was posted to *Cappellini*, whose original commander, Masi, had just left for the newly established school at Pola.

*Cappellini's* gun-battle with a British destroyer in the Straits has already been described. In the autumn of 1940 she made the passage again under Todaro's command. There is no point in going into details, which would only be repetitive. It is enough to say that Todaro, like others, reached the Atlantic after twenty-four hours of adventurous navigation below the surface. Then began the usual long, weary patrol in bad weather, the unremitting search for a target, which had to be carried out on the surface, no matter what the conditions, lest any chance of sighting an enemy should be missed. At last, after a fortnight at sea, a distant silhouette was picked up one morning at dawn. Todaro attacked. His target, as he discovered later, was the Portuguese ship *Cabalho*, then under charter to the British, with a cargo of crated aircraft. He attacked boldly on the surface, as he always did, using his guns rather than torpedoes. This method of attack was typical of Todaro and earned a caustic comment from Doenitz in the margin of one of his reports: "It is a pity that this officer is not commanding a gun-boat." It was not kindly meant; but it was a tribute, all the same, to a certain quixotic vein in Todaro's character.

The *Cabalho* sank quickly after a short fight of the kind which became commonplace during the war. There would be no need to say any more, if it were not for Todaro's subsequent actions. The story is worth telling, if only in outline, because it made quite a stir at the time, both in Italy and abroad. What happened, in short, was that Todaro, like Leoni before him, was faced with the painful problem of what to do with the crew of the ship he had sunk. Should they be left to take their chance in the ship's boat or taken on board *Cappellini* during the weeks when she would still be at sea? Todaro's whole character was against the first solution and the second was physically impossible. So he adopted a third, which was to take the boat in tow for nearly 600 miles across the Atlantic. It meant exposing himself and his command to a serious risk by sailing at reduced speed on the surface, an easy prey to enemy destroyers and aircraft. But he did it and duly brought *Cabalho's* crew to safety, only dropping the tow when they were within sight of land.

This episode brought Todaro a severe rocket when he got back to Bordeaux. From the operational point of view it was richly deserved. But one would not be sorry to see more people earn rockets of this kind, in peace as well as in war; it would strengthen one's confidence in the human race. Even at the time, Todaro had supporters as well as critics. People he had never heard of—including some from enemy countries—wrote to him in gratitude and admiration. I saw one of these letters; it was from a Portuguese woman who saluted him as an "angel of goodness" and *"chevalier sans peur et sans reproche"*. It was not a bad description.

A couple of months later, after a rest and a thorough re-fit, *Cappellini* left again for the Atlantic, this time for a particularly difficult billet off West Africa. I remember seeing her when she sailed. She looked like a racing-car, stripped for an event, with all superfluities removed. She had taken on extra fuel and was lying very low in the water with her casing almost awash. Her two four-inch guns were shining and her conning-tower was stripped of all its hamper. Her crew, lined up on the casing in their greys, looked proud of their boat and her captain. Each of them had a dirk in his belt. Looking at these, someone suggested that Todaro's plan was to carry enemy ships by boarding, like a buccaneer. But those who knew him better saw the point. The dirks were not a brag nor a boy's thriller version of modern war, but an emblem designed to raise the morale of the crew on a difficult operation. The only man who carried no arms at all was Todaro himself. So far as I know, he never did —an appropriate gesture from a man of his character and outlook.

*Cappellini* left for her billet three thousand miles to the south, in an area where, up to December 1940, no German or Italian submarine had operated. It was a virgin field, but one of vital importance to British trade, where surprise would be the essence of the attack. The first few days of the patrol were without incident. Winter in the Bay of Biscay was succeeded by spring off Rio di Oro and then by summer off Senegal. The first brush with the enemy occurred off Cape Verde and took the form of an action on the surface with the armed merchant cruiser *Aeumeus*, of seven thousand tons. *Cappellini* soon beat down her defence and sank her. Her next encounter, about the latitude of Freetown, was with another auxiliary cruiser, the *Shakespeare*, of eight thousand tons, then acting as a troopship. She had three four-inch guns and a number of quickfirers and was evidently under the command of a gallant and energetic captain.

The action began about eight in the morning and was fought in Todaro's characteristic style on the surface. This time *Cappellini* had a tough and dogged opponent; and the duel, which lasted about four hours, was hard-fought on both sides. When Todaro opened fire, the *Shakespeare* hit back with her four-inch guns and tried to break contact. *Cappellini* gave chase and, having a higher surface speed, was able to close to point-blank range. The Englishman redoubled his defence. *Cappellini* was swept by shell and machine-gun fire and her gun-crews suffered heavy casualties. But engineers and engine-room ratings, released from duty below, clamoured for leave to join in the fight. Among them was Lieut. (E) Stiepovich. He saw the machine-gunner fall and asked for "the honour of taking his post". The phrase might have come out of a storybook, but I have quoted it exactly. Permission was given and he took the gunner's place, only to be seriously wounded himself by a shell splinter. He refused to be carried below because, as he said, he wanted to be in at the death.

At last, about noon, the *Shakespeare*, riddled by gun-fire and hit by at least one torpedo, caught fire and sank. Meanwhile, in reply to an S O S, a British aircraft from Freetown had appeared on the scene. Todaro made an emergency dive; but the first aircraft was soon followed by others and then by corvettes and other anti-submarine craft. A furious hunt was up, which lasted all that day, all night and all the day following.

Below in the submarine, where he had been carried when they dived, Stiepovich was in agony, but made no complaint. All he asked was to see the ship's flag before he died; and Todaro left the control-room for a few minutes to spread it out before him. This again sounds like a scene from a book—a book written in the days before chauvinism had taken a grip on the world. But it was in fact a scene from real life between two men to whom the words "country" and "flag" had a more than rhetorical meaning. Its setting was a submerged sub-marine, shaken by depth-charges and already in serious danger from damage sustained in earlier fighting.

Thanks to the skill and steady nerves of her captain and crew, *Cappellini* made good her escape. But when she finally reached Bordeaux, she was little better than a wreck. Four months' work was needed to put her into shape again.

After completing three patrols in the Atlantic and sinking some 25,000 tons of enemy shipping, Todaro took a holiday. That is to say, he transferred to the naval Commandos and was given the job of raising and train-ing a flotilla of midget submarines, which were intended for operations in the Black Sea. I caught a glimpse of his patient, meticulous work when I was at Spezia, fitting out the *Da Recco* as a convoy escort. Todaro was there too with his one-man submarines of the B and C types and we used to meet to discuss our mutual problems. It was the last time I saw him. I found the same fresh enthusiasm, the same fighting spirit, which had struck me at Bordeaux, the same habitual kindness and a com-plete absence of that carping outlook which did us so much harm during the war. I don't imagine that Todaro had missed the obvious weaknesses in our wartime organi-sation or the dangerous paralysis which gripped our strategy; but he rarely mentioned them and never dwelt on them.

In the spring of 1942 he was busy with his midget submarines to the exclusion of everything else. He tackled the job with his usual enthusiasm and, when everything was ready, transferred himself and his force overland to the Black Sea. It would be interesting to write an account of this landward navigation of tractor-borne midget submarines; but we must pass that over. I will only say that the Italian craft, based on Foros in the Yalta area, fought and sank a number of enemy ships. Todaro was always in the van either with the submarines or with the assault-boats (*barchini*)[1] with which he raised hell, as on the occasion of the feint-attack which he staged at Balaclava to cover a German landing elsewhere.

Todaro returned from the Black Sea to the Mediterranean, this time in command of a detachment of *barchini*, using a steam-trawler as their parent-ship. She was an odd craft for the job; but in wartime Italy everything went into the stockpot and the personnel of Special Forces were adepts at finding a use for everything that floated and every device that could be turned against the enemy. Todaro's trawler was the *Cefalo*. A few months before she had been fishing in the Gulf of Taranto. Now she was fitted with cradles on deck to carry a pair of *barchini*; the whole affair was camouflaged with fishing-nets; and she became a formidable ship of war.

The method of operation was as follows. *Cefalo* tramped the Mediterranean, a dirty and innocuous piece of old iron, with a fine display of fishing-nets on deck. As soon as an enemy was sighted, the nets disappeared and the *barchini* slipped into the water and raced for their target. *Cefalo's* function, in fact, was to provide living-quarters for the pilots and to transport the assault-boats to areas which they could not have reached under their own power.

[1] i.e. MTM or modified speedboats. They were flat-bottomed boats with outboard motors, capable of thirty-two knots. They carried 600 lb. of explosive in the bows which was fired either on impact or by water-pressure. They were one-man boats; and it was the pilot's job, when he was about 100 yards from the target, to aim the boat, lock the steering and drop off himself into the water. Another type, the MTSM, carried a torpedo which the helmsman could fire. These were the only assault-boats used, apart from the MAS.

In December 1942, Todaro was operating in the Narrows—much as one would expect, since that was then the busiest theatre of war at sea. An operation was laid on for his forces against Bône, which the enemy were then using as an offensive base. It was a difficult and dangerous affair, and miscarried for reasons which there is no space to go into here. Its indirect result was the death of Todaro, one of the bravest men and most determined fighters in the Italian Navy.

It is possible, since he was not without psychic gifts, that Todaro had a premonition of the end. He told one of his officers that he felt a strange inward disturbance; but he played his part in the operation with his usual dash and persistence. On the morning of 14th December, when *Cefalo* was homeward bound, he threw himself on his bunk to snatch an hour's rest after a night of action. Fate chose that moment to intervene, hoping perhaps to catch an old warrior off his guard. Her instrument was an American aircraft, which she brought down to sea-level and aimed, so to speak, at the unprotected trawler. A burst of machine-gun fire riddled the deck-house and hit the sleeping man in the forehead. He was found with his lips still parted in a faint smile. So died Salvatore Todaro, the knight errant, a very brave and great-hearted man.

## Chapter VI

## ATLANTIC INCIDENTS

THE two of our submarines which most resembled U-boats in their original design were *Argo* and *Velella*. They were small, built on workman-like lines without too much superstructure, and only lacked speed to make them ideally suitable for commerce-raiding in the Atlantic on the German pattern.

*Argo* had returned from Eritrea just before the war, and was ready for sea after a short refit, when it became necessary to find a new Commander. As she belonged to the Spezia flotilla, it fell to me to propose Lieut. Crepas, then second-in-command of the mine-laying submarine *Micca*. He later showed himself fully up to the job both in seamanship and fighting spirit. *Argo* was among the submarines transferred to Bordeaux; and the following story illustrates both the grimness of the struggle in the Atlantic and the errors that are possible in night-fighting.

In the winter of 1940, *Argo* was on patrol in the N. Atlantic looking for a target, when she received a signal from *Betasom* giving the position of a convoy and ordering her to attack. She set a course at once to intercept the convoy, though it was clear from their relative positions that she could not do so in under twenty-five to thirty hours at full speed. She finally reached the indicated position at night, only to find the familiar tragic evidence of a fight that was already over. Flames lit up

46

the scene. Some ships were on fire, others sinking; wreckage of all kinds was strewn about; and the water seemed full of survivors. These men, even if they were picked up by lifeboats, would still be at the mercy of the sea, with little food and water and no protection against the weather.

It was a sight to wring any heart; but what could be done? It is needless to repeat that survivors could not be taken on board a small submarine, least of all one with several weeks' patrol ahead of her. Nor could there be any question of taking boats in tow in prevailing conditions in the N. Atlantic.

*Argo* worked her way among the boats for a while, handing out food, medical stores and clothing. Then she turned back to her search for a target. It was an anxious, meticulous search, for so far we had had few successes in northern waters and had come in for some not very genial criticism from our German allies. *Argo* accordingly put all she had into the search; but there was no doubt that the battle—or that phase of the battle—was finally over. There was no undamaged ship in sight; even the U-boats had left the scene. Nor was there any sign of the convoy escort, which should still have been in the area, if only to search for survivors. When he was certain that he had drawn a blank, Crepas set an easterly course in search of a more promising hunting-ground. No sooner had he done so than something—something moving very fast—loomed up out of the night. He guessed rather than saw that it was a destroyer, a submarine's worst enemy; but he went straight in to the attack—in the circumstances, of course, on the surface. The range was calculated in a few seconds and two torpedoes fired at the moving mass. *Argo* then withdrew at full speed and, as she did so, felt the percussion of two explosions. It was an undoubted hit; with two torpedoes in her belly the destroyer could confidently be written off.

But Crepas, wanting to make sure, turned back in his tracks, keeping a sharp look-out for wreckage, survivors or perhaps even a sinking ship. A long search produced nothing except, finally, a few bits of flotsam and a considerable quantity of papers and log-books scattered over a wide area. These were gathered up and from them Crepas learnt that his victim had been H.M.C.S. *Saguenay*. As no other trace could be found, he inferred, reasonably enough, that she was a total loss and had left nothing behind except her identity-card, so to speak, in the form of part of the ship's papers.

It was an important success. Crepas congratulated himself and went on with his patrol. He sank a merchantman by night on the surface after an attack initiated by his Number One, de Santis, who was in charge of the bridge while he was getting some sleep; and then, being low in fuel, turned for home. *Argo* was almost in the Bay of Biscay when an incident occurred which threw a gloom over an otherwise successful cruise. The blow came not from the enemy but from the sea, from the storm-bound Atlantic, whose violence tried our men's endurance to the utmost. A wave, steeper than usual, swept de Santis overboard. *Argo* hove-to and began an intensive search, quartering the whole area without result. It was not weather in which anything could live. After twenty-four hours the search was abandoned and *Argo* returned to *Betasom*, where she was greeted by congratulations for her success and sympathy for her loss.

The next day *B.d.U* asked for confirmation of the sunk destroyer's identity and the name *Saguenay* was repeated.

48

But there was evidently something wrong. A few hours later we were told that *Saguenay* had been reported homeward bound to her base in Scotland. Signals flew between *Betasom* and the *B.d.U* and finally we were shown some intercepted enemy signals, from which it appeared that *Saguenay*, her bows shot away, had been taken in tow by another ship and was creeping towards the British Isles at about three knots. The next report showed her almost home and surrounded by aircraft, tugs and escorts. Alas for the claims of Crepas and the crew of the *Argo*!

It must be admitted that British ships had tough skins, if two torpedoes were not enough to finish them. But much the same was true, on occasion, of certain Italian destroyers.

A number of men were lost overboard from our Atlantic submarines, especially during the early months. Each time it happened, the ship's company came back not only grieved but somehow diminished, as if the loss of a man at sea, and the failure to rescue him, had struck them a collective blow. Losses by enemy action, however sad, were easier to accept; but in fact there were few single casualties. If the enemy scored a direct hit, it was generally the whole boat that went. But one such incident is worth recording, for in it the Navy lost a keen and courageous officer of an old Service family, Sub.-Lieut. Carlo Marenco di Moriondo.

He was a young man, just out of the Naval College and fervently patriotic. He was killed in action on *Glauco* and buried at sea, where his heart was and where family tradition had led him. It was in a night action against a small, unescorted merchantman, an action which seemed insignificant at first, but proved otherwise, when *Glauco*, having missed with her torpedoes, opened fire with her guns. In most actions of the kind, the merchantman's crew abandoned ship and took to the boats, but in this case the fire was returned and not without success. Marenco, who was officer of the watch, seeing that the enemy's shots were falling close, made up his mind to bring the after-gun into action as well as the forward one, which was the only one then firing. To save time and ensure an accurate aim, he went to lay the gun himself. He ignored the enemy's well-aimed fire and had, I am sure, no thought in his mind but to do his duty and make his contribution to a victory. He brought his gun into action and had fired one or two rounds, when an enemy shell sprayed the deck with splinters and killed him. The brief episode was over; and *Glauco* dived to escape a fire which had now become too hot.

I said above that a total of thirty-two Italian submarines operated in the Atlantic. So far we have only seen twenty-seven through the Straits of Gibraltar. To complete the tally we must add *Cagni* and four submarines from the Red Sea. The latter's story is well known. When Massawa was about to fall, *Guglielmotti*, *Ferraris*, *Archimede* and *Perla*, the only surviving submarines in the Red Sea, were ordered to transfer to Bordeaux by the Indian Ocean and the Atlantic. They thus avoided Gibraltar and only had to tackle the less difficult problem of the Perim passage. On the other hand, they were in a low state of efficiency, partly as the result of twelve months in tropical waters and partly because of the isolated and increasingly precarious position of their late base. Nevertheless, all four reached their destination—though after certain adventures on the way—including the little *Perla*, classified in all naval directories as a "short-range submarine". From Massawa to Bordeaux she had to cover a good

14,000 knots in all and was twice refuelled at sea by German tankers. But she got there.

*Cagni's* story was very different. She was built and fitted out between 1941 and 1942 expressly for ocean warfare. As soon as she was commissioned, she left the Mediterranean via Gibraltar, completed a successful patrol in which she sank three ships, and arrived safely at Bordeaux. This completes our total of thirty-four passages through the Straits.

By the summer of 1941 it had become clear to us at *Betasom*—and still more to the *B.d.U*—that, despite the alterations which had been carried out, some Italian submarines would never be fully efficient for Atlantic operations. These it was decided to repatriate. Accordingly eleven submarines were sent back to the Mediterranean that summer and again passed the Straits one by one, though this time with different and clearer orders. Ten of them made the trip successfully, bringing our total score to forty-four. The eleventh, *Glauco* (Lieut.-Cdr. Baroni), did not get through. But it would be wrong to attribute her loss to the passage of the Straits, for it happened in an action 250 miles to the west. She was surprised on the surface by a British destroyer and dived at once. But her enemy, H.M.S. *Wishart*, had marked her down and after a four hours' hunt, straddled her with a well-placed pattern of depth-charges. The result, according to the verbal account we had from one of the few survivors, was to spring a number of leaks in the hull, fuse the motors and damage the batteries. *Glauco* faced a problem with only two answers—to go down as she was or try a last desperate battle on the surface. She chose the second and came up. She received some hits as she surfaced, but managed to clear away her own gun. Then she was swept by another burst of shell and machine-gun fire; several of her crew were hit; and *Glauco* up-ended and began to sink. Further shots, perhaps aimed at the submarine, killed a number of men in the sea. Finally, when *Glauco* slid out of sight, *Wishart* picked up the survivors, including *Glauco's* commander.

This was our only loss in the many operations in which Italian submarines forced the Straits of Gibraltar.

## Chapter VII

### *TORELLI'S* CAREER

THE hero (or heroine) of this story is not a commander, an officer or a rating but a ship—to be more precise, a submarine. As everyone knows who has spent any time at sea, ships, though officially classed as inanimate objects, are in fact no such thing. No sailor would dare to deny that his boat has a brain, a career and a personality of her own. The same is true of a warship; and no one who fought at sea between 1940 and 1945 would think to question it. Sceptics may be referred to certain significant episodes in the Battle of Cape Matapan, about which I shall have something to say later. For the moment we can concentrate on the wartime career of one particular ship with a mind of her own—the submarine *Torelli*, whose passage through the Straits has already been described. She was one of the bravest and most faithful of Italy's submarines. She spent three eventful years in the Atlantic and then, in the summer of 1943, motored without any fuss from Bordeaux to Singapore. In the end she found her grave in the China Sea; but it was, you may say, a natural death, for the principal characteristic of this remarkable boat was her capacity for bringing her crew safely back to port.

*Torelli* was very young at the outbreak of war, indeed scarcely born, for her final trials did not take place until

August 1940. She would then have liked a working-up cruise, an opportunity to find herself and settle in her machinery and her crew before she took to the high seas. But this was not allowed. Other intelligences did not foresee that a young submarine might like to do a little sailing in home waters before she took on her war-work in the ocean. I shall not make any comment on this policy except to say that no German submarine was considered operational until she had worked up for three months in the Baltic.

*Torelli,* on the other hand, left for the Atlantic as soon as she had run her final dockyard trials. She had a rather elderly commander, in his forties, who had not served in submarines for some time, a crew which had not yet shaken down and one officer—he joined her just as she was casting off—who had never been on board a submarine before. (He later became *Torelli's* last skipper.) Nevertheless, she negotiated the Straits, as I have described, and carried out a good month's patrol off the Azores. Fate was not particularly kind to her and presented her, among other things, with a young cyclone, which caught her head-on. But she came through it all handsomely enough and arrived in Bordeaux at the beginning of October, a little knocked about, but having established her reputation for reaching port, whatever opposition she might meet from the enemy or the weather.

She fetched up in Bordeaux again in July 1942 under Bruno Migliorini's command. That time she had caught it good and proper, but she made her port nevertheless. True, it took her six weeks; but the important thing in such cases is to get there. I won't set out all her adventures in detail, which might end by being boring. But the high-lights were as follows. She was bombed from the

air; her batteries caught fire; she stranded on Cape Penas[1]
and got herself off and out of neutral waters within the
legal time-limit; she was attacked again by Sunderlands
and seriously damaged; she took refuge in Santander,
carried out repairs in the harbour and escaped while
Spanish tugs were actually bringing her in to the quay.
Finally, she made Bordeaux on 15th July 1942.

As I say, she always got home. She had even managed
to do so early in 1942 after a heavy and prolonged attack
by ships and aircraft. She was then under Antonio De
Giacomo's command, serving off the Brazilian coast, and
was straddled by several sticks of bombs at a moment
when, as luck would have it, she could not dive. She
lost two men—Coxswain Pallucchini and Telegraphist
Lubrano, both killed by bomb splinters while serving
the A.A. gun. (They were *Torelli's* only casualties during
the whole war.) But in return she shot down one aircraft
and hit another and was able to finish her patrol, in the
course of which she sent a tanker to the bottom. *Torelli*
had previously sunk other ships while under De Giacomo's command; but her most brilliant exploit was
under Primo Longobardo, who later died heroically on
*Calvi,* and was posthumously awarded the Gold Cross.
Between 5th January and 6th February 1941, *Torelli* was
on patrol in the North Atlantic and performed the feat
of destroying single-handed a complete, if small, enemy
convoy of four ships. The whole action, from the marking
down of the convoy to the actual fighting, occupied forty-
eight very tense hours; but the result was one of our most
conspicuous single-ship successes. On her way back to
base, *Torelli* suffered the inevitable pursuit by an enemy
hunting-group but, in order to finish her patrol with

[1] In northern Spain.

an air, succeeded in sinking a fifth merchantman on the way.

A brilliant action, well-conducted by a brave captain; but it was not in battles that *Torelli* really showed at her best, so much as in patient, methodical operations of a different kind. When she had to fight, she did so with complete confidence, as she had for Longobardo and De Giacomo, but her strongest suit was getting out of difficulties which would have proved fatal to any other submarine. One can see the skill she showed under Migliorini in getting clear of the enemy and escaping internment; but the best example of all is her long and hazardous voyage from Bordeaux to Singapore under Lt. Groppallo's command—the same officer who had joined her in 1940 as she was casting off. This was *Torelli's* last voyage and one which extended over eleven weeks. But a detailed description must wait for another chapter, because it involves the adventures of other submarines and the outcome of a skilful and complex operation.

## CHAPTER VIII

## PITTONI AND THE *BAGNOLINI*

THE Italian Navy achieved its first success of the war on the night of 12th June 1940, when the submarine *Bagnolini* torpedoed the British cruiser *Calypso*. To tell the truth, this episode, which occurred less than forty-eight hours after the outbreak of war, made very little noise at the time, even perhaps in naval circles; and there are not many people who remember it. But it was an action in which one does not know what most to admire—the boldness and precision with which it was executed or the skill and clearheadedness of the captain, Lt.-Cdr. Franco Tosoni Pittoni. I say "clearheadedness" on purpose because previously there had been a good deal of confused thinking in the Italian Navy about the possibility of night-attacks by submarines. Tosoni, however, knew exactly what he was about, either by day or by night. He knew instinctively because he had been ten years in submarines and understood the potentialities of his weapon. Consequently, when one night he sighted a British cruiser squadron, he stayed on the surface and concentrated on closing the range as much as possible, despite the presence of the destroyer-screen, the most deadly enemy that a submarine can have.

*Bagnolini* closed up in the way that one should always do, especially in a night-action. When she was within a few hundred yards of the British squadron, she fired her torpedoes and dived to escape the counter-attack, which developed at once. But Tosoni, knowing his position in relation to the enemy, was certain that he could not have missed. It took about thirty seconds for the sound of the torpedoes' explosion to reach the submarine. Some days later the crew of *Bagnolini* learnt that they had sunk the *Calypso*, the first of the twelve cruisers which the British lost in the Mediterranean between June 1940 and September 1943.

For this action Tosoni was awarded the Silver Cross— one of the few cases in which the sinking of an enemy warship did not win the Gold Cross. Later, having transferred to the Atlantic with *Bagnolini*, Tosoni made a fresh name for himself as a commerce-raider. But his most severe test came in December 1940, and was one from which he emerged with great credit, though at the cost of severe damage to his submarine. It was another proof of the exceptional gifts of seamanship and command possessed by this slightly built enthusiast, who looked even younger than he was and won the hearts of both his men and his superior officers.

All this, as I said, was in December 1940. The first intimation that *Bagnolini* was in serious trouble reached *Betasom* in the form of a cipher-signal from Tosoni, in which he reported that his submarine "had damaged her batteries and was making a good deal of water; her compass was also out of action, but he had set a course to the south...." At the time when this signal was received, *Bagnolini* was known to be on patrol off the south coast of England, so that her position appeared to be extremely grave, if not desperate. The only redeeming feature was the statement that she was heading south and must, therefore, still have her diesels in action. She could not dive and had no electricity and no compass; but she could still move. That was something—enough at any rate to keep a little flicker of hope alive at *Betasom*. Moreover, Tosoni's first message did not end there. He added the information that he had sunk a merchantman, an auxiliary cruiser and, possibly, a destroyer.

It did not require much penetration to see what had happened. Tosoni had evidently attacked a convoy and sunk one merchant ship and an escort and had then faced a counter-attack, all the heavier because he had chosen to pick off his victims at the very entrance to the lion's den.

At *Betasom*, *Bagnolini's* signal was studied at once; but there was not much help that we could give. Tosoni was ordered to try to make St. Jean-de-Luz, plotting his course as best he could. Next morning the Germans agreed to provide an escort of aircraft and M-boats[1]; and the whole southern coast of the Bay of Biscay was alerted. On the following day the weather was so bad that the German search failed to pick up the submarine. But that night a further signal was received from Tosoni to the effect that he hoped to make St. Jean-de-Luz by dawn. And it was in that small French port that I first heard the story of his adventures.

Late one afternoon he had sighted an enemy convoy and given chase. That night he attacked and scored hits with his torpedoes on two British ships, which later proved to be a merchantman and an auxiliary cruiser. So far everything had gone smoothly; then, as *Bagnolini* was disengaging, the British escort got on her tail and a hunt began, which lasted for a day and a night.

Tosoni, as I have said, knew his job and had his boat well in hand. He dived to a good depth and then, relying

[1]Fast minesweepers.

59

on his hydrophones, began a complicated pattern of manœuvres, darting this way and that and making frequent
changes of speed and depth. The British destroyers stayed
over *Bagnolini* the rest of the night; and by dawn they
had been reinforced by aircraft. The search continued
with increasing intensity all that day and the following
night. Meanwhile, conditions on board *Bagnolini* had
been getting steadily worse. She was making water, having
started several rivets and opened at least one seam; and
her batteries were flooded and were giving off chlorine.
She could no longer hold her depth and had to come up
to forty-five, to forty, to thirty fathoms. The lighting-
system had failed and her rudders were beginning to give
trouble. The end seemed very near.

But Tosoni had no intention of going down like that,
like a rat caught in a trap. It was better to surface, even
under the noses of enemy destroyers, and face the un-
equal battle which would follow and die with some éclat,
rather than prolong the slow agony below. So *Bagnolini*
came up. The diesels started more quickly than they
had ever done; the guns were cleared away in a few
seconds and the torpedo-tubes loaded. Two destroyers
loomed up astern, very close, and Tosoni fired a parting
salvo of four torpedoes before setting his course for the
south. He had a distinct impression of having scored a
hit; but the loss was never officially confirmed, so we must
write it off here as a possible. There is no doubt that
Tosoni's final thrust disorganised the opposition and
threw them temporarily off balance, for *Bagnolini* was
not attacked again, perhaps not even followed, as she
made her get-away. But she was now in such straits
that Tosoni despaired of bringing her home safely. This
was the point at which he sent his signal. He knew well

PITTONI AND THE *BAGNOLINI*

enough that he could expect little help and must rely on his own resources; but he made his signal all the same, perhaps to report his success, perhaps simply because it gave him a link with *Betasom* and so with home. He did not put it like that when he made his verbal report to me; but one could read something of the kind in his expression and on the faces of the ratings standing round.

*Bagnolini* went in for repairs. Her commander, after a long leave, transferred to *Bianchi*, a newer boat, faster and better armed than *Bagnolini*. But *Bianchi* went missing on her next patrol. We know now that she was torpedoed, homeward bound in the Bay of Biscay, by the submarine *Severn* on 7th August 1941.

## CHAPTER IX

## TRAMPING TO SINGAPORE

A NYONE who saw *Cappellini* leave La Pallice, north
of Bordeaux, on 11th May 1943, would have had
great difficulty in guessing that this strange floating object, heading out to sea, was really a submarine on
the surface with her diesels going flat out. All that could
be seen was a hump moving through the water, which
only the initiated could have recognized as the bow of a
submarine, and then, some way astern, the outline of the
bridge, bristling with all the bits and pieces which a self-
respecting submarine carries around with her. This would
have been more easily recognizable, even without the
periscope standards and the aerial of the *Metox*[1] sticking
up beside the loop of the direction-finder. Abaft the
bridge everything was under water. So was the fore-
casing except for the extreme point of the bows; so was
the after-casing and the engine-room hatch; so was the
gun-platform, though the gun itself had been dismounted;
so were the exhausts of the diesels, down which, if the
engines had stopped suddenly, half the sea would have
tipped.

Very few people would have recognized an Italian submarine in these two humps moving slowly through the
waters of La Pallice. Still less would they have thought
that the submarine was sailing at her full surface-speed

[1] An apparatus which showed the presence of radar operating in the area.

and with the intention of covering a good 13,000 knots (or, say, 25,000 km.) in this extraordinary trim across two oceans entirely dominated by the enemy. But this marine phenomenon was in fact *Cappellini*, stuffed like a crocodile with an odd assortment of cargo, and under orders to sail from the west coast of France to Sabang in Sumatra, and thence to Singapore, exactly half-way round the world.

In all, seven submarines were earmarked for this difficult voyage, carrying much-needed materials to our Japanese ally, and returning with an equally valuable cargo for our own war industry. But of the seven, only five actually started. *Cappellini* was the first to leave and, as we shall see, made a record trip. She was followed by *Tazzoli* on 16th May; *Giuliani* on 23rd May; *Torelli* on 14th June; and *Barbarigo* on 15th June. Five Italian submarines sailing under German names—*Cappellini* became *Adler 3*—because the operation was on German account, though the commanders and crews were all Italian. On their arrival in the Far East our boats were to report to *Eritrea*, an Italian sloop which, under Iannucci's command, had slipped out of Massawa in 1941 for Indonesia, under the noses of British cruisers and Dutch aircraft, eluding the former by a little luck and more skill, and deceiving the latter by the judicious use of a few tins of paint and a dummy mast. On 8th September 1943 the same ship, in obedience to orders, waved goodbye to the Malayans, Japanese and Germans at Singapore and, taking advantage of rain-storms and fog, ran the Straits of Malacca at the reckless speed of ten knots and emerged undetected in the Indian Ocean.[1]

[1] *Eritrea* later served with the Royal Navy in Indian waters. (Tr.)

Between May and June 1943, as I said, five Italian submarines, converted from warships into slow and inoffensive merchantmen, left the French coast. Only three —Auconi's *Cappellini*, Groppallo's *Torelli* and Tei's *Giuliani*—reached their destination. *Tazzoli* and *Barbarigo*, two names famous in our submarine history, never made Sabang or any other port, but were lost without trace like so many of their fellows. Even to-day, after consulting British and American records, no one knows exactly when or how they were lost. *Tazzoli* is thought to have been sunk by a British aircraft in the Bay of Biscay on 16th June, the day she left the Gironde; but the loss of *Barbarigo* remains a mystery. Perhaps she was sunk by aircraft, perhaps by another submarine, who later disappeared herself; perhaps, since anything is possible, she was simply wrecked.

The idea of using Italian submarines for blockade-running between Europe and the Far East originated, so far as I know, at *Betasom*, when the then Captain S/M, Capt. Enzo Grossi, reluctantly decided that the seven submarines still at Bordeaux were no longer fit for commerce-raiding. Grossi reported in this sense to Admiral Doenitz in February 1943, adding his opinion that to go on using them in this way was to send them to certain death. He asked instead if he could put Italian crews into seven of the new German U-boats. This was not such an odd request as it sounds, for the Germans, who were then launching one U-boat a day, were short of crews, whereas we had a surplus of crews for the boats we still possessed or were able to build.

Doenitz agreed with Grossi's proposal at once, but made the condition that *Betasom* should convert the Italian submarines at Bordeaux into cargo-boats for use between

Axis-controlled Europe and the Far East. There was a vital need for traffic of this kind, for the Japanese were desperately short of mercury, alloy-steel and medical stores, which Germany and Italy could supply, while the Axis was equally short of Far Eastern tin, cotton and rubber.

In the conditions of 1943 it was no longer possible to use ordinary merchant-ships. In the two previous years some Italian motor-ships, of which I shall say more, had succeeded in running the blockade with mercury and arms for Japan, cotton and rubber for Europe. But after the arrival of *Orseolo* at Bordeaux in the spring of 1943, no other merchant-ship had been able to risk the voyage. Consequently, if any trade were to be carried on at all, it had to be by submarines, which could, if necessary, escape the enemy's attentions by submerging.

This was the origin of the deal by which Germany handed over seven efficient U-boats to Italian crews and we in exchange converted our remaining submarines— still manned and commanded by Italians—to cargo-boats on the Far Eastern run. The agreement was, of course, scrupulously honoured on both sides. *Betasom* sent off her boats to Singapore as and when they were ready; and Doenitz, on his side, regularly shipped Italian crews in the U-boats under orders for Bordeaux. In fact, on 8th September, these ex-German submarines were just about to sail for their new base, while *Bagnolini* and *Finzi*, the last boats of the Atlantic Flotilla, with their cargo on board, were on the point of leaving for Singapore. But then the Armistice intervened and cancelled all agreements.

Let me say at once that submarines make shocking cargo-boats; but so would any warship or anything else, for that matter, which was used for a purpose for which it was not designed. To make the point clear, I must explain that the maximum cargo which could possibly be crammed into the largest of these converted submarines was 150 tons on the outward voyage and 190 tons on the homeward voyage, which did not in fact take place. How small a cargo this was can be seen by making a comparison with an ordinary small merchantman, or tramp, which would normally carry 3,000 or 4,000 tons.

The 190 tons loaded by *Giuliani* at Singapore for her homeward voyage was an outside limit, only made possible because she expected to refuel at sea. The normal cargo was 120 to 150 tons or even as little as 95 tons, which was all that *Cappellini* succeeded in loading at La Pallice. True, it was a valuable cargo of alloy-steel, mercury in bottles and cases of munitions, but still only 95 tons. To underline the point I will add the list of what *Cappellini* took on board at Singapore: 92 tons of rubber; 54 of tin; 5 of tungsten; 4 of opium and quinine—a total of 155 tons with rather less fuel than on the outward voyage because, like *Giuliani*, she expected to refuel at sea.

I have already said that in these cargo-carrying submarines the guns were dismounted. In fact, the whole armament was stripped, partly to make room for more cargo, partly so as to remove any temptation which the skippers might have had to fight. Their job was to carry their 100 tons of cargo to the other side of the world— that and nothing else. If they met an American aircraft-carrier or an English troopship, they were to let them go, without even reporting their positions, because at that moment tin, mercury and rubber were more important than all the aircraft-carriers and troopships in the world.

The only guns left on board were the A.A. machine-guns on the bridge, and they were of little use against the big, long-range British and American aircraft. All the other armament had been removed, torpedoes put on shore, ammunition lockers converted to fuel tanks (with the inevitable result of oil-leaks inside the submarine) and torpedo-tubes turned into storage space. One section of batteries had also been removed, so that the boats' speed and handiness under water were much reduced. Every inch of space that could be found was crammed with cargo, extra fuel or stores. Bunks disappeared and so did the cubby-hole dignified on submarines by the name of Captain's cabin. Two of the lavatories were scrapped, leaving only one for the whole crew, and with them went everything which could be classed as a comfort —showers, cupboards, locker-space, etc. It is difficult to visualize how much room can be taken up by 95 tons of cargo, 260 tons of fuel and food and fresh water for 50 men for three months—for even men who are pre-pared to work under the most difficult conditions still have to be kept alive.

The result was chaotic: men slept squeezed between a case of sphaghetti and a bottle of mercury; the electric cooker was mounted on a pile of tinned vegetables; and the bars of alloy-steel were used as a platform from which to inspect the hydraulic gear.

*Torelli* had an additional problem of her own in the shape of a passenger—the Japanese Lieut.-Col. Kinze Saterke, who was going home after learning all that the Germans could teach him about wireless. He brought seven suitcases with him, as mysterious as they were large, which evidently contained Top Secret docu-ments and apparatus, for he refused to be parted from them during the whole of an adventurous two months' voyage.

Enemy aircraft and destroyers made a dead set at *Torelli*. They were on top of her from the moment she poked her nose out of Bordeaux and did not let go until she had passed St. Helena. The original team from the British Isles handed her on to another from Gibraltar, and that team to one from the Azores, supported by partners from Cape Verde. Then came destroyers, corvettes and every kind of mischief from Freetown, from Ascension and finally from St. Helena itself. But *Torelli* was a remarkable submarine with a particular gift for shaking off corvettes, frigates, Sunderlands and Catalinas. She lived up to her reputation once more and was able to show the Japanese Colonel how an unarmed Italian submarine, out of trim and very unhandy when submerged, could still defeat a fierce and systematic hunt. She had, of course, to take an evasive route, spend several days longer at sea than she had intended and, what was worse, exceed her estimated fuel consumption by a fairly wide margin. As the result, she ran out of fuel in the middle of the Indian Ocean, despite the extra load she was carrying and all the care taken to keep consumption down. If she reached Sabang at all, it was only because she fell in with a German U-boat from whom she was able to take on enough fuel to make port. And so *Torelli* reached Sumatra with her Japanese Colonel and his secret papers, her steel ingots, bottles of mercury and a few gun-mountings.

Let us now return to *Cappellini*, whom we left pulling out of the little harbour of La Pallice with no more than her bridge and the tip of her bows showing out of the water. Her engine-room telegraphs said Full Speed

Ahead; but, given her weight and trim, full speed meant something between six and seven knots at most. Pulling was about it. In this state she reached the open sea just in time to catch an air-attack, the first of a long and weary series.

In the early part of the war a submarine attacked from the air, if well-armed and under good control, usually stayed on the surface and fought it out with her opponent. But by the summer of 1943, I doubt if any submarine commander would have had the slightest wish to try conclusions with the aircraft that were flapping round him. There were too many of them for one thing, and all their vital parts were well armoured; for another, they were equipped with a gyroscopic bomb-sight, which made it almost impossible to miss. For a submarine as badly armed as *Cappellini* and only floating by a miracle, to have accepted battle would have been practically suicide, so Auconi ordered a rapid dive.

I ought now to go into various complicated explanations to show why a submarine, which is already down by the stern, cannot dive as quickly as she should; but it is better to skip the technicalities. What cannot be skipped, however, is the jet of water which found its way in through a weak joint as soon as *Cappellini* reached a certain depth. Nor can we pass over the cargo, which lurched about all over the place as soon as her fore and aft trim was altered. When that sort of thing happens in the ordinary way, one blows a ballast-tank and everything returns to normal. But *Cappellini* was carrying a minimum of ballast to make more room for fuel and cargo and, if she had got rid of any of it, her bridge and her bows would have broken surface again. To get back onto an even keel, she had to bring some of her crew forward

Madeira, inviting the inevitable air-attack and a hunt by British corvettes from the Cape Verde Islands and Freetown. Then, sailing partly on the surface and partly submerged, she reached the Equator unscathed, thanks to a good deal of luck and some cover from a tropical rainstorm. "A symbolic douche of sea-water," says the log, "for those who had not crossed the Line before and a nonsymbolic douche of bombs from aircraft probably out of Ascension. On 13th June we were off Cape Town, passing less than forty miles from that base."

The orders said three hundred miles; but it was a good thing that *Cappellini* ignored them, for she reached Sabang with no more than two hours' fuel remaining.

There was a time in the days of coal-fired boilers and before Pullino[1] had thought of submarines, when a Captain who found himself short of fuel could give the traditional order to burn the cabin furniture or even the woodwork of the bridge and thus bring his ship happily into port. But on *Cappellini* it would have been difficult to persuade the diesels to digest aluminium furniture or iron deck-plates. Since there was nothing in hand but the oil in the reserve tanks, Auconi managed very well. So, for that matter, did Tei in *Giuliani*, who only just made it by following the prescribed route, a fact which did not prevent him from running into a very heavy attack, south-west of Madeira, from a flight of aircraft who pounced on him out of a fog-bank.

At this point I may remind any reader who has forgotten that by 1943 all British and American aircraft operating on the high seas or in the Mediterranean were equipped with radar, which could spot a submarine on

[1] Giacinto Pullino (1831–1897), Piedmontese engineer, who built the first Italian submarine, the *Delfino*.

the surface at a range of fifty miles, and, of course, worked just as well at night, in the thickest fog or the heaviest tropical rainstorm. The submarine, on the other hand, had no warning of the flock of birds of ill-omen who were about to swoop on her. Or rather, she had eyes when she could use them—that is, on a clear day—and what someone called that damned suave, the *Metox*. This instrument was supposed to give warning when radar was in use in the area; but it sometimes failed to work and, worse still, was itself detectable on a radar screen.

Off the Cape *Cappellini* struck a westerly gale—one of the kind which keep aircraft tucked up in their hangars and corvettes in harbour with their moorings doubled. It put the old boat to a very severe test. Auconi reported afterwards that they had been fortunate in having a following sea. No doubt he was speaking relatively, for he added: "The whole of the after-casing, including the engine exhausts, carried away. Men on safety-lines worked feverishly, with seas constantly breaking over them, to cut away loose plates which were threatening to enlarge the damage already done. Then the gale increased and became almost more than we could stand. We were taking water right over the bridge and down the hatch, which was the only air intake for the diesels. More water was coming into the control-room than the pumps could deal with. This continued for over a week. We carried out repairs as best we could, partly on the surface and partly submerged. At a depth of forty fathoms we had a ten-degree roll. Diving and surfacing were delicate operations and obviously dangerous, especially as the batteries were spilling large quantities of acid."

I have given this extract in full because there are times when bald, official prose is worth any amount of fine writing. I need only add that, after a month at sea, life on board was better organized than when *Cappellini* set out, if only because the oil in the torpedo-tubes and ammunition-lockers had been used up and a good quantity of stores consumed. Consequently there was more room to move about and one could do so without getting covered with oil. On the other hand, a certain amount of sea-water had inevitably fetched up in the batteries, where it was generating chlorine gas, most of which ended in the crew's lungs, since the forward and the after hatch were still under water and the ventilating system was behaving in a very unorthodox way. By 20th June *Cappellini* was in the Indian Ocean, having crossed the Atlantic from north to south at a time when the U-boats were suffering their worst losses of the whole war and Italy was reporting missing the submarines *Morosini*, *Archimede* and *Da Vinci*. On 9th July she entered the port of Sabang in Sumatra, where she was greeted by *Eritrea* and by the Japanese Lt.-Cdr. Yoshida, locally known as the King of Sabang. Three weeks later *Giuliani* arrived and on 26th August *Torelli*. All three were immediately taken in to Singapore by *Eritrea* to unload their cargoes, carry out necessary repairs and re-load and re-victual for the homeward voyage.

At this ex-British base—captured intact by the Japs, who found enormous stocks of food, fuel and munitions —endless discussions went on between the Italian Commander Iannucci, the Japanese Admiral Enamoto, the German Von Zatorsky and the skippers of the three submarines. One party wanted to mark time, the other to hurry up the turn round. In the end only *Cappellini* was ready to sail by the beginning of September with a fine cargo of 155 tons of rubber, tin, quinine and opium,

together with as much fuel as would take her to the point
in the South Atlantic where she had a rendezvous with a
U-boat for refuelling. But even *Cappellini* never left the
Far East.

When the Armistice came on 8th September, she was
at Sabang just about to leave. *Giuliani* and *Torelli*—the
latter having arrived a bare week before—were still at
Singapore, loading and refitting. All three were interned
and then, when their Italian crews had been marched
off to a camp, were taken over by the Germans. *Giuliani*,
already the *Adler 5,* was re-christened U(IT)23 and was
lost on 14th February 1944, when the British submarine
*Tallyho* torpedoed her in the Malacca channel. *Torelli*
and *Cappellini* were later handed over to the Japanese by
the Germans when they too began to feel the pinch.
Their end came when the Americans scuppered them off
Kobe in the autumn of 1945.

# PART II

## ADVENTURES IN UNIFORM

### CHAPTER X

### INVADING CRETE

FROM Bordeaux I was transferred to Leros in the Ægean. To tell the truth, my job at *Betasom* had never really appealed to me and I had been pressing for an active command. By that I did not mean the command of an island in the Ægean, but a sea-going appointment, preferably in destroyers. But the Admiralty having pronounced otherwise, I had no choice but to obey. Accordingly, I set off by air for Leros, or rather for Rhodes, because it was some time before I got as far as Leros itself. You will see why in a moment. But first I must say something about the flight from Italy to the Dodecanese, partly because of an incident which occurred on the way, partly because the first pilot of the aircraft was my brother Enzo, a major in the Air Force Reserve.

Enzo, a veteran of the air, had been a civil pilot and was recalled at the outbreak of war with the rank of Captain. His first job was to fly the three-engined transports which were ferrying dismantled fighter-aircraft from Rome to Asmara. It was a long and dangerous route, three-quarters of which lay across enemy territory.

For this work Enzo was promoted and given the Silver Cross. During 1942 and 1943 he worked hard—indeed, over-worked—flying in supplies to our forces in Libya, Tunis and Pantelleria. He was able to carry out all his assignments successfully, but in the process badly over-strained his heart. When he took up intensive flying again in 1950 it would no longer stand the strain and finally gave out while he was flying as Captain of one of *Alitalia's* four-engined aircraft.

At the time of which I am speaking, he was on the regular service between Italy and the Ægean, so it was not difficult for me to arrange to fly with him. As it was years since we had had the chance of spending a few hours together, accident and our respective careers having kept us apart, the meeting was more than a pleasure to both of us. The plane's second pilot was Lt.-Col. Fortunato Federici, another veteran and much decorated. He was later killed in action in the Ægean, over the island of Amorgos, at the end of 1941.

We were flying over the Corinth Canal—incidentally a prohibited area—and were all very happy, when, about noon on 20th May 1941, we sighted a dense formation of German aircraft, escorted by fighters. Our course was easterly, while they were heading south, so we soon left them behind, without any of us being able to guess what their destination was. The incident did nothing to disturb our enjoyment of the flight, which went on as calmly and peacefully as a pleasure-trip. We landed on schedule at the airport of Gadurra in Rhodes in the late afternoon; and here we found the answer to the problem which had puzzled us on the way. It was D-day for the German attack on Crete; and the planes we had seen were carrying the assault-troops to

Maleme and Retimo airfields on the western end of the island.

Everyone remembers that it was a bitterly contested operation. What is more often forgotten is that an Italian sea-borne expedition also took part. It landed in eastern Crete on 28th May; and it was thanks to this landing that the Germans later handed over to us the control of that end of the island. Please do not laugh at the memory of this little operation. It is true that the convoy which sailed from Rhodes on the afternoon of 27th May looked more like a Walt Disney film than a highly organized amphibious force. Indeed, I doubt whether a stranger assortment of floating objects ever set out to attack a strongly fortified island across seas which, despite the activities of our aircraft, were still dominated by the enemy. But it was not a joke. The little argosy reached its destination under the noses of a British squadron; and the 500 seamen and 2,500 troops on board were landed safely and occupied the corner of Crete between Sitia, San Nicola and Hierapetra. Even the four hundred pestilential mules which accompanied the expedition reached land safely, with one exception. This mule was thrown into the sea with the rest off Sitia—our methods of disembarkation may have been rather crude—but refused to swim ashore, setting a northerly course instead, perhaps with the idea of returning to his stable in Rhodes. We also landed the expedition's stores—five days' rations and ammunition—part of which was dumped at Sitia, while the rest followed the troops by sea as they moved westward from their landing-point.

What more do you want?

I agree that there were no striking deeds of valour during the voyage and that no one won the Gold Cross.

But there are times when the truest courage is not to fight, if fighting means inevitable and total destruction. That was roughly our position; nevertheless, we defeated, if only in the sense of eluding, a British cruiser squadron, which would have swallowed us whole if they had caught us. And that was what mattered. Of course, as we should have been the first to admit, the fact that everything went off perfectly was largely a matter of luck—something to off-set the many times when luck had run the other way

At this point I must go back again to the beginning. It is not necessary to re-tell the story of the German invasion of Crete; but the reader must be reminded that between the 21st and 25th May the German air-borne troops were only just holding their initial positions round the airfields of Retimo, Maleme and Heraklion. In the meanwhile the two convoys, carrying the sea-borne sup-porting force, had been destroyed or dispersed by British ships, despite the great courage displayed by the escorting destroyers, *Lupo* and *Sagittario*. It was at this point that our authorities in Rhodes began to play with the idea, which had been in their minds since the beginning, of taking part in the operation with an Italian brigade.

Since an Italian air-borne assault was out of the question, the plan from the outset was for a landing from the sea. True, we did not then possess any specialized land-ing-craft, either in the Ægean or anywhere else; but this was in 1941, when some romance still hung about the war and men were supposed to be able to triumph over machines. The authorities in the Dodecanese thought, perhaps, that we were still living in the days of Garibaldi. At any rate, the miscellaneous collection of boats des-cribed above was all that they considered necessary to transport a military force across the Ægean. As it turned out, they were right: the little boats did their duty and reached their destination. But I must add that this was not the result generally expected at the time, if one may judge from a certain shyness in making local craft available. The D.Q.M.G. would not allow us to take his tug, *Apuania*, in case she should be lost; nor would H.E. the Governor let us have his *Lepanto* for the same reason. We were also refused the old *Caboto*, then stationed at Rhodes, because she was still carried on the Navy's books as a cruiser and no one wanted the enemy to be able to claim the loss of such an important ship, if the expedition miscarried.

In fact, these three ships would have been very useful: the first for her carrying capacity, the second for her guns and the third for her efficient W/T apparatus. But they all had to be left in port; and the expedition's commander—handsomely styled for the occasion, Naval Commander-in-Chief—had to be content with a few fishing-boats, a couple of tugs and so on. When they had been assembled, he drew up the following list for the benefit of future historians:

4 motor fishing vessels (*gazolini*): *Sant'Antonio, Navigatore, Plutone* and *San Giorgio*. Splendid names, but maddeningly slow boats.

2 steamships: *Orsini* and *Tarquinia*. Good, but very small; *Orsini* wore the C.-in-C.'s colours.

1 river-boat, *Porto di Roma*. She came from the Tiber and had been transformed into a tank landing-craft, no less.

2 refrigerated ships: *Addis Ababa* and *Assab*. Tiny and with quite useless holds.

1 lagoon-steamer: *Giampaolo*. Anyone who has been to Venice will know what that means.

2 tugs: *Aguglia* and *Impero*.

3 tankers: *Nera* and two others, which were little more than petrol-lighters of the kind normally used in harbour.

Fifteen boats in all with a speed of between six and nine knots and none of the equipment necessary for landing on an enemy coast. The fishing-boats and tankers had indeed been fitted with patent ramps, which the inventor fondly believed could be used for landing; but as they were unable to get near enough to the beach, their ramps remained sadly hanging from the bows, while the troops, if they wanted a dry landing, had to use the motor-boats, dinghies and whalers which we had fortunately towed from Rhodes to Sitia.

Please do not misunderstand me. The light-hearted things I have said so far do not take away the significance of the operation or detract from the courage of those who took part in it, well aware of the risks they were running. Yet our greatest difficulty was to persuade a few people to stay behind in Rhodes; and, even so, at the last moment we found that we had a number of stowaways.

The force embarked on our fifteen little ships was made up of men of the 9th Infantry Division, supported by the thirteen light tanks (very light, I thought) in the *Porto di Roma*, some Blackshirt detachments (among whom I remember Terragni, the mayor of Como) and a company of Carabinieri. The C.O., Colonel Caffaro, also disposed of two cars, a small truck and the four hundred mules already mentioned—our supply services could hardly be called mechanised. Under the Naval Commander came two companies of seamen, whose task was to establish and defend the base while the infantry and "A.F.V.'s" rumbled into the interior.

So much for the preparations for our amphibious operation. As for its execution, I think I have said already that we sailed from Rhodes on the late afternoon of 27th May. Nothing of note happened that night except that there was a fresh north-westerly wind and enough swell to empty the rations out of the Infantry and Blackshirts. Next day was fine and calm and everything returned to normal. When the fleet-destroyer *Crispi,* the escorts *Lira, Lince* and *Libra,* two E-boats and a few fighters formed up round the convoy, the C.-in-C. began to feel that Nelson, dashing for the West Indies after Villeneuve, had little on him. No doubt it was this idea which suggested to him that he might abandon his prescribed route altogether and set a course direct for Sitia, whose half-dozen houses were his final goal. The original route had been worked out with the idea of keeping the convoy close to land so that, if anything went wrong, the troops would at least have a reef to hang on to. This was a good idea in itself, but one which was bound to waste a good deal of time; and it was for this reason that our neo-Nelson decided to forget about islands and reefs and head straight out to sea. It was fortunate that he did so because, as we shall see, it was precisely the few hours saved by the new course which enabled him to bring his command safely to Sitia.

At 1300 hours on 28th May the log of the little flagship showed "Nothing to report". In the circumstances it was the best and most hopeful entry that there could have been. Until 1300 hours, therefore, all was well; but then a signal from Rhodes changed our "All Clear", if not into All Wrong, at least to something pretty near it. The signal informed us baldly that three cruisers and six destroyers of the Royal Navy had been sighted in the

Eastern Mediterranean on course for the Ægean at full
speed. They were heading, to be exact, for the Straits
between Crete and the island of Caxo, which we were
due to cross within the next few hours. It was our reconnaissance planes which had reported the British ships,
and, since their names are now known, they may as well
be given. They were the cruisers *Orion, Ajax* and *Dido,*
and the destroyers *Decoy, Jackal, Hotspur, Kimberley,*
*Imperial* and *Hereward,* Rear-Admiral Rawlings commanding. Three cruisers and six destroyers—not bad for
fifteen small boats escorted by *Crispi,* three escort-
destroyers and two E-boats. But to tell the truth, Admiral
Rawlings was not after the 9th Infantry; his only object
was to reach the north side of Crete and give support to
the British troops who were still holding out. But you
know how these things go. If the Admiral had happened
to meet, right across his path, a number of fishing-boats
and petrol-lighters bulging with troops, he would certainly
have improved the occasion with a little target-practice.

On board *Orsini* we plotted our own and the enemy's
position on the chart; and even a blind man could see
that the British ships, if they continued as they were
going, would be off Sitia by 1700 hours. No one objected
to that in principle, but it happened to be the precise
moment which we had selected for our own arrival. What
could be done? We were already sailing at the maximum
speed of the slowest ships in the convoy—some of the
very slowest had even dropped behind. We were taking
the shortest route; and we had the largest escort which
our forces in the Ægean could supply. We could, of
course, have turned to port and run for the island of
Scarpanto, which was not far away. But the war, as I
said before, was still in its romantic phase. We therefore

held our course for Sitia without bothering too much about the presence of *Orion, Ajax* and the rest. And in fact, though we did not know this at the time, we were steadily gaining on them, thanks to the activities of the German and Italian airforces in the Ægean.

In the event, the C.-in-C. proved to have been right to trust to luck and everything worked out well, as the following rather scrambled entries from *Orsini's* log will show:

1330 hrs. Ordered all boats to increase speed. This made a lot of smoke without raising our speed by as much as half a knot. Tug *Impero* a long way behind.

1500 hrs. Admiral signals from Rhodes suggesting we increase speed. We had thought of this already.

1515 hrs. Ordered escort *Lince* to take *Impero* in tow and bring her up with us. *Lince* disappeared over horizon and was seen no more.

1545 hrs. *Crispi* also disappears, having received orders from Rhodes to shell the lighthouse on Cape Sidero.

1600 hrs. Learn from intercepted signals that German-Italian aircraft have attacked enemy squadron. But indicated position suggests that they have not reduced speed.

1615 hrs. Entering Sitia bay. Two of our escorts leave us under orders from Rhodes, but *Crispi* rejoins.

1650 hrs. Opening the beach. No reaction from on shore; village apparently deserted. I order all boats in to the beach.

1700 hrs. Boats of the convoy beach themselves as instructed. *Giampaolo*—lagoon-steamer carrying some three hundred men—ties up at the wooden wharf by the quay. *Crispi* stands by to beat down any opposition with her

4-inch guns; but everything still quiet on shore. Tanks from the *Porto di Roma* clamber down the ramps and occupy covering-positions ashore. Seamen from the landing-parties go ashore and are told off to rig temporary jetties, man the ship's boats which we have towed with us, and organize a ferry-service.

1720 hrs. All 3,000 men of the expeditionary force are ashore and starting their march inland. Unloading of stores begins.

While all this was going on, the British squadron found themselves in a very awkward position. Their difficulties lasted for two or three hours and slowed them down a good deal more than either Admiral Rawlings or Sir Andrew Cunningham, who commanded the Mediterranean Fleet from Alexandria, could have foreseen. It appears from Sir Andrew's memoirs—a reliable source— that *Orion* was under heavy air-attack during the whole afternoon of the 28th; *Ajax* was hit by Italian torpedo-bombers of 281a Squadron and obliged to turn back; and the destroyer *Imperial* was also attacked by a formation of S.84 bombers. Despite this, Admiral Rawlings held on his course, though at reduced speed. Between 2100 and 2200 hours he was at last off Sitia, probing the coast with searchlights and gunfire for something which was indeed there, though he failed either to find or to hit it. We can only be grateful to him, as also for the fact that he did not waste much time over these tedious evolutions under our noses. His object, as I said before, was not to chase Italian landing-parties, but to evacuate the British garrison; and with this in view he presently made off to the west after firing a few rounds in our direction and into Mirabella Bay.

86

By dawn next day, however, cruisers and destroyers were once again off Sitia and again under air-attack, this time by Stukas, one of which dropped a bomb down the destroyer *Hereward's* funnel and broke her in two. After this the British went off for good, leaving our E-boats to pick up the survivors. But even their return journey was not clear of trouble. The air-attacks continued on their way back to Alexandria and resulted—again according to Cunningham—in serious damage to the destroyer *Decoy* and then in succession to the cruisers *Dido* and *Orion*. In all, of the nine ships which left Egypt on the evening of 27th May, only three—the destroyers *Jackal*, *Hotspur* and *Kimberley*—returned unhurt.

As soon as they had landed, Col. Caffaro's infantry and tanks fanned out and occupied positions on the hills surrounding Sitia Bay. This was obviously the right course. The two companies of seamen remained behind in the deserted village, where they set up the nucleus of a supply-base and took over various suitable buildings as stores. It was not a very grand affair. Everything was on a modest scale as befitted the poor relations which we were and remained throughout the war. But it was necessary to organize some sort of base, through which supplies could flow in from Rhodes; and for the moment the most convenient point to do so was the beach on which we had landed. Most of the seamen were assigned to the defence of the perimeter. The remainder, with a few officers landed from the ships, became what could be called (with a little imagination) Naval H.Q., Crete. The Commanding Officer was *Betasom's* late Chief of Staff. He had with him Lt. Pucci as second-in-command; Lt. Sanguinetti in charge of the beach and the naval landing-parties; Aiello as Port-Captain; and Lt. Montanari as

Quartermaster. The last-named had the biggest job, for it fell to him to issue rations and stores to the five hundred men who remained at Sitia.

A field-bank was set up, against the time when currency should reach us and an invitation issued to the inhabitants to return home with the promise that no one would hurt them. Gradually those who had taken to the hills on our arrival filtered back, at first rather diffidently, then more trustfully and finally with complete confidence as they discovered that Italians, even when disguised as invaders, could never manage to look very fierce. With that the story of our landing in Crete is really over. The enemy's furious resistance died away rapidly[1] and ceased altogether within a few days of our landing at Sitia. The Italian brigade, moving from the east, made contact with the Germans at the junction of the San Nicola–Hierapetra–Heraklion roads and then took over San Nicola while the Germans occupied Hierapetra. Our base at Sitia was also transferred to San Nicola and remained there until the end of the war. Its original C.O. was replaced by Commander Giuseppe Orlando and then continued his interrupted journey to Leros by seaplane.

[1] The decision to evacuate Crete was taken on 27th May, the day when the Italian expedition left Rhodes. (Tr.)

## CHAPTER XI

## THE ATTACK THAT FAILED

THE more one thinks of the defence of Tobruk against the British attack on the night of 13th September 1942, the more one admires the cool heads of the commanders, who were able to do so much with a handful of men and a few motor-barges.

Improvisation is an over-worked word. If I must use it here, it is only in the sense that a chronic shortage of equipment obliged Italian forces to improvise throughout the war, even in the most carefully planned operations. In this particular case, General Giannantoni, the fortress-commander, had worked out elaborate plans for the defence of Tobruk. But—a "but" familiar to all Italians who served in the war—these plans depended on the existence of a number of men, guns and vehicles that were not forthcoming either in or near Tobruk. Consequently, when the British attack came, it was improvisation rather than a well-thought-out tactical plan which defeated it.

It was not an easy problem, for the fortress came under simultaneous attack from land, sea and air, by sea-borne troops, by commandos and by the Long Range Desert Group, of which Lord Montgomery was so justly proud. Let me add in parenthesis that Montgomery's book, *Alamein to the Sangro,* contains no mention at all of this bold operation, of which, had it been successful, so much hours when an air-attack began in quite unusual strength. It continued at the same intensity until 0300 hours. Meanwhile all our guards and picquets had been alerted. D'Aloja, still preoccupied with the submarine, also turned out the motor-barges and stationed them along the boom-defences and off the more vulnerable beaches. No one else would have considered turning these transport boats into efficient instruments of war; but it turned out to be a happy thought, for they later put up a very good show.

Nothing further happened until midnight. It had begun to look as if an intruding submarine and a heavy air-attack were all that was intended, when the main attack developed and we began to see what the British were after. Just on midnight a report reached Naval H.Q. that units of the Long Range Desert Group, mounted on trucks, had penetrated the outer defences from the land-ward side, made contact with commandos landed from assault-boats at Mersa Shusc, south of Tobruk, and cap-tured a 4-inch battery. So far the enemy's operations had gone according to plan. But when the LRDG and the Commandos attempted the next step—the capture of the naval 6-inch battery further south at Mersa Biad—things began to go awry, because the battery not only refused to be captured, but gave the general alarm to the fortress.

Lombardi, D'Aloja and Battaglia thus had a fairly clear picture of what was happening on the south side of the bay. The only troops available were one company of the San Marco naval battalion—120 seamen under Lieut. Colotto—which they sent at once to Mersa Shusc. Other units of the San Marco battalion were already posted along the coast and came into action (very successfully) where they were. But there was no other reserve on which H.Q. could draw.

Apart from the LRDG and the Commandos, the British plan also provided for *Sikh* and *Zulu* to land about 400 marines on the north side of the bay at approximately 0100 hours. This was the landing-point which the submarine should have marked. So it did, but none too well, since our anti-submarine craft had driven the intruder at least three miles north of his intended position. Consequently, when the landing-parties from *Sikh* and *Zulu* got ashore, they found themselves in the middle of the desert instead of on the outskirts of Tobruk. Moreover, they bumped into an outpost—the one known to us as Fort Perrone—which gave the alarm, so that H.Q. were now informed of both arms of the attack. But when they looked round for some troops with which to meet the threat from the north, they were forced to realise that, now the San Marco company had gone, there were none left. They took the appropriate action; that is to say, they collected cooks, storemen, orderlies and headquarters clerks, German or Italian, added a few *carabinieri* and bundled them off to the threatened point. This scratch team included forty seamen, forty *carabinieri* and thirty German soldiers, who had reported for duty of their own accord. On the way, the party was joined by another fifty *carabinieri* under the commander of the 18th CC. RR. Battalion. To the north, then, went 160 men collected at random; to the south the 120 seamen of the San Marco battalion. Nothing was left at H.Q., where a local defence had been organised in case the attack should penetrate right into the town, except sixty seamen and twenty-five men of the Italian African Police.

The order of battle of the defence was not imposing— very much the reverse. Yet it was those 160 cooks, orderlies, etc., who held the position in the north against the

400 marines from *Sikh* and *Zulu*; and Colotto's 120 seamen who pinned down the Commandos and the LRDG
to the south of the naval 6-inch battery, and so enabled
that battery to open a well-directed fire on *Sikh* and *Zulu*
as they were withdrawing at dawn. Both ships were
sunk.[1] A notable part was also played by the quick-firing
batteries on the south side of the bay and the 4-inch
Dandalo battery, another Naval post, which was not yet
operational but managed to bring two guns into action
with crews drawn from the artificers who were mounting
the battery. The cruiser *Coventry*, supporting the operation from a distance, was sunk by German and Italian
aircraft.

But the real high-spot of the defence—one might even
call it a masterpiece—was the behaviour of D'Aloja's
motor-barges when a group of British MTB tried to force
the boom-defences. The barges were awkward boats to
handle—perfect clowns in the water—but, armed with
light cannon and a few machine-guns, they turned themselves into formidable opponents, spouting fire like the
Roman candles of our youth. The enemy found barges
at Mersa Shusc and off all the beaches where they tried
to land. Had they got so far, they would also have found
them alongside all the wharves in the harbour. But the
largest concentration was along the boom-defences, where
between 0100 hours and 0600 hours a series of hand-to-
hand battles developed between the barges and the enemy
MTB. The barges manœuvred with the precision and
hitting power of torpedo-boats, despite the air-attack
which continued throughout the night, the confused posi-

---

[1] The boats landing her marines not having returned, *Sikh* moved inshore
in search of them and was disabled by gunfire at 5.30 a.m. *Zulu*, having
attempted unsuccessfully to tow her off, rejoined the supporting force; later
she and the AA cruiser *Coventry* were both sunk by air attack. (Tr.)

tion on shore and at sea and the difficulty of maintaining any central control.

Before striking a final balance, I must add that Admiral Lombardi, as soon as he became aware that a major attack was developing, sent off dispatch riders—the telephone-lines had been cut—to General Diendl and to the Italian command under which Tobruk came, with requests for support. Diendl arrived in person at ten o'clock the following morning, but only to kick up a frightful row because we had had the impertinence to defeat the British without waiting for him. G.H.Q. dispatched some *Bersaglieri* contingents from Bardia, but these arrived too late to join in the fun. We did, however, receive one reinforcement in the shape of Admiral Girosi and General Ferrari, who jumped into a truck as soon as they heard the news and drove straight for Tobruk with an escort of two *carabinieri* armed with tommy-guns, with the idea of acting as a liaison with G.H.Q. or, at any rate, joining the party themselves. I must also award an honourable mention to Signalman Zinni, who found the British operation-order with its details of all the nice (or nasty) things that were going to happen both at Tobruk and further down the coast. In fact they did not happen, partly as the result of a spirited local resistance and partly, I think, because the knowledge gained from the captured plan enabled the defence to deploy its limited resources where they were most needed.

The final balance-sheet ran as follows: destroyers *Sikh* and *Zulu* sunk by the Tobruk batteries; cruiser *Coventry* sunk by air attack; at least six MTB and many landing-craft destroyed by motor-barges; *MTB 314* captured intact; over 600 prisoners, including the force commander. Italian losses: about 50 men all told.

## Chapter XII

## THE *KASBAH*

FELTRINELLI exchanged a few words, perhaps a password, with the old man and then followed him towards the outskirts of Alexandria. The old man was small and skinny, with a grey walrus moustache; his linen suit and panama were shabby and yellowish. The two walked on in silence until they reached the door of an isolated villa, hidden away among palms and casuarinas.

For Feltrinelli this was the prelude to a month of complete unreality, a grotesque film-script made up of scraps of Graham Greene, Robert Hichens and Buchan. It was the spring of 1942; and he spent his month in the heart of an enemy city under the eyes of the police, not lurking, but living high, wide and plentiful.

Luigi Feltrinelli was an attractive chap, fair, well-made, athletic and a bit of a cynic. He spent his war as the pilot of an assault-boat, carrying out the most reckless and dare-devil operations, only to die after the Armistice in a tragic but quite ordinary accident. I knew him first in Massawa in 1939, when he was combining the duties of engineer on the *Nullo* with the less austere but equally heavy job—when you consider the climate—of captain of the destroyer's football team. We met again in Leros in December 1941, when the Alexandria operation was

96

An encounter between an Italian submarine and a British destroyer.
  (Top): The submarine caught in a searchlight.
  (Centre): The prize crew on board at daybreak.
  (Bottom): A small boat from the destroyer alongside the sinking submarine.

An Italian submarine returning to its base.

An Italian cruiser in action in the battle of Gaudo.

being planned.[1] He and the other pilots were our guests on the island while the submarine *Sciré* was stationed there before her successful mission. Feltrinelli took part in that operation as a supernumerary, his only job being to lend a hand when the others pushed off from *Sciré* and headed towards the enemy base. But in the repeat operation of May 1942 he had an active part, which led in the end to his extraordinary adventures in the *Kasbah*.

Once more I will skip the operational details, in particular details of the improved defence which the British had organised after our coup of the previous December. It is enough to say that in May 1942 things went less smoothly. Some trick of the current carried the submarine *Ambra*, under Arillo's command, off her course and hampered what was in any case a very delicate operation. As a result none of the three human-torpedoes was able to penetrate the harbour, not even the one piloted by Feltrinelli with the diver Favale as his number two. The pair coasted for some hours along the low-lying, marshy shore of Alexandria looking for some point of entry to the Naval Base. But in the end, under fire and shaken by under-water explosions, they decided that there was no hope of reaching their objective. They destroyed their *pig*[2] and landed about 3 a.m. right in the middle of the dockyard.

Feltrinelli decided not to give himself up, but to play possum instead in the hope of gaining time and perhaps organising an escape back to Italy. He took off his diving-suit and sank it and removed the rank-badges from his overalls. (Pilots always wore uniform under their diving-

[1] On 18th Dec., 1941, three Italian "human-torpedoes" penetrated the defences of Alexandria and fixed delayed-action mines to the hulls of the *Queen Elizabeth* and the *Valiant*; both ships were seriously damaged.
[2] Nickname for human-torpedoes, see page 103.

dress so that, if captured, they could claim the status of
P.O.W.s.) He hoped that his clothes, which were shabby
enough, might enable him to pass as a dockyard hand.
He took up this part when he saw that the night shift
was ending and joined the stream of other workmen who
were drifting sleepily towards the dock-gates. A casual
nod to the sentry and he was through and at large in
Alexandria.

Our Secret Service was never as good as the British;
but after two years of war it had managed to set up a
certain organisation, especially in Middle Eastern ports,
which were always full of Italians. The rendezvous in
Alexandria was in the park, where one could usually be
certain of picking up a contact, if the occasion warranted
it. It was there that Feltrinelli entered his unreal world.

The isolated villa to which he was taken contained a
woman, a gorgeous blonde, who in the best film tradition
fell in love with him, supplied him with clothes and
money and found him a hide-out in the *Kasbah*. There
he lived for rather more than a month in an extraordinary cosmopolitan world of spies, thieves and black-
marketeers.

If this had been all, it would have been queer enough
though nothing out of the way, for thousands of people
at one time or another must have hidden up in the
*Kasbah*. But Feltrinelli's story had an added twist. The
blonde had no intention of keeping her protégé tucked
away in the Arab quarter. She wanted him by her side,
moving in the same circles as she did—that is to say, the
best society in Alexandria, the most exclusive clubs and
all the grandest parties. Feltrinelli had to embark on a
double, or, rather, treble life, dividing his time between the
villa, the *Kasbah* and the café society of Alexandria. He

played his part to perfection. He made friends, squired old ladies, played bridge à la Culbertson at the best tables, drank the King's health at semi-official dinners and sat puffing an Egyptian cigarette and telling smoking-room stories after the ladies had withdrawn. He heard the confidences of the most tightly buttoned of high officials; he allowed certain elegant fingers to ruffle his hair; and, in the intervals, he drank thick coffee among Levantines bartering sacks of rice for rubber balls or selling cotton for piastres, dollars, sterling or rupees.

But all good things must have an end. One day the police surrounded the *Kasbah*; it was said that they were searching for an Italian officer. Feltrinelli saw that the game was up, put on his overalls again with the rank-badges restored, and surrendered to the N.C.O. in charge of the picquet. He spent the rest of the war in a P.O.W. camp.

CHAPTER XIII

VILLA CARMELA

THE Villa Carmela—"Italy's very advanced naval base in enemy waters", as Valerio Borghese called it[1]—has been so often filmed and written about that the subject may well seem exhausted. Yet it is still worth while to say something more, if only to put the story back into its proper perspective. I should like to get rid of the thriller-writing and romance and come back to the facts, the real story of how this little white villa, hidden among the greenery of Puente Majorga, was converted into an offensive base only half a mile away from the British shipping in Gibraltar harbour.

Of course, there was a great deal of romance. Imagine a typical Spanish villa housing a newly-married couple. The husband is Antonio Ramognino, an Italian, apparently of no occupation beyond a little fishing. His wife is the shy, retiring Conchita, who is recuperating in the Straits because her nerves have suffered in wartime Italy. The Governor of Algeciras is an occasional visitor at the villa; and outside, as often as not, stands the mysterious, though easily identifiable, "Mr. Perrera". And from the villa Italian frogmen secretly emerge to plant mines on British merchant ships.

Where could you find a better background for a thriller? It was so good that journalists and script-writers have felt

[1]In his book *Decima Flottiglia Mas*.

bound to add just that little more which makes the whole thing fantastic. But that was not a mistake which the actual organizers could afford to make. In fact, the whole operation was worked out with the same painstaking logic as a mathematical theorem; and the romantic accounts of the journalists—among which I include the article by a French Admiral in *Hommes et Mondes*—have left out the best part of the story. How did the swimmers get to the Villa Carmela? And how was the villa stocked with all the requirements of a self-supporting base—diving-suits, aqualungs, explosives, limpet mines and all the rest?

Borghese, it is true, gives some account of this in his book; but he has left himself no space to linger over the details. He omits the episode, for instance, of Ramognino's arrest when his passport was out of order. Not that the passport mattered very much in itself; but it would have been awkward if the police had found the heavy automatic hidden in his Peugeot runabout. . . .

To start at the beginning: Antonio Ramognino, who came from Genoa, was more than a newly-wed and apparently idle husband with no thought except for his wife's health. He was also the originator and chief of the whole project, so that a Spanish police enquiry, however it started, might well have had disastrous results. It would have meant the internment of Antonio and Conchita, the closing down of Villa Carmela and a sad end to a very promising operation. However, he was able to get out of it that time by giving the name of Conchita's uncle, a high official in Madrid. After a couple of telephone-calls, nothing happened but a small fine for having his papers out of order. No one, thank heaven, noticed the pistol.

But the real story starts rather earlier, on the day when Ramognino first submitted designs to the Admiralty for a new naval weapon. There is no need to describe his early plans and calculations or the process by which an honest instrument of war was converted into a project bristling with official stamps, seals and serial numbers. The file went the usual rounds from one office or department to another, from Genoa to Spezia, from Spezia to Rome, from Rome to Levanto, until one day it fetched up in the hands of Moccagatta, who was then commanding the 10th Flotilla MAS.[1] He saw the importance of the invention at once, but was too busy planning his bold but ill-fated operation against Malta to be able to do anything about it. He wrote to Ramognino from Augusta, where his headquarters then were, saying that he would go further into the matter as soon as he got back to Spezia.

This was, in fact, one of the last letters that Moccagatta wrote, for he was killed by machine-gun fire from an aircraft during the attack on Malta. I mention it only to show another facet of this remarkable man, who could find the time to give serious thought to a new weapon, while planning an unimaginably difficult operation.

Moccagatta's death was a severe setback to Ramognino. In the summer of 1941, experiments were carried out on the beach at Levanto, though it was not until September that a meeting at Spezia between Ramognino, Borghese and Todaro set the project on the right path. Or nearly the right path because, in fact, that particular invention was never used against the enemy; but the contact with Borghese and a further inspiration by Ramognino led to the Admiralty decision to rent a villa on Spanish soil near Algeciras and use it as a base for undercover operations.

[1] Motor assault boats. (Tr.)

Borghese, who knew from experience how difficult and dangerous it was to launch frogmen or human-torpedoes from a submarine riding on the surface of the Straits, gave the plan his warmest approval. He enlisted Ramognino, who was graded as unfit for service, as a volunteer in the 10th Flotilla and sent him and his wife off to Spain to look for a villa.

Antonio and Conchita entered Spain on 6th April 1942 in a blaze of publicity. They travelled round the country in a car conspicuously labelled "Italian Mission", stopping in hotels where their arrival was always heralded in advance. But they managed to carry out their mission all the same with the invaluable help of a certain Doctor Falasco, who had previously lived in Algeciras, but had moved at the outbreak of war to a villa about five miles away.

We shall meet Falasco again. For the moment let us follow Antonio and Conchita, who found and rented near Puente Mayorga just the little villa which Conchita's health seemed to require. They also interested themselves in the Italian ships which were being repaired in Algeciras or were lying half-submerged in the harbour, where they had been scuppered at the outbreak of war. There were three or four of them, including the *Lavoro*, the *Pagao* and the *Olterra*. It occurred to Ramognino that one of these, suitably equipped, would complete the base which he was planning to set up at the villa. Under cover of repair-work, she could be fitted out with all the apparatus necessary for preparing and launching the complicated assault-craft known officially as SLC's or slow torpedoes, but popularly called *pigs*. This was work which could not possibly be done at the villa.

The Ramogninos returned to Spezia, where Borghese at once approved the plan to set up not one but two operational bases within range of Gibraltar: the first on the tanker *Olterra* for the human torpedoes; the second at Villa Carmela for the frogmen.

Much has already been written about the *Olterra* and her crew—the famous *Ursa Major* team—and I shall have something to say myself in a later chapter about *Olterra's* commander, Lieut. Licio Visintini, who sacrificed himself in Gibraltar harbour. But now we must concentrate on the Villa Carmela, which, though part of the same organisation, formed a separate unit on its own. The Villa opened for business at the beginning of June, 1942, as soon as the honeymoon couple were installed.

"We ordered a lot of furniture," writes Ramognino, "much more than was needed. We got it a little at a time from widely separated places and it was delivered in lorries which used to make long stops at Falasco's house on their way."

Falasco's house, you will remember, was out in the country and, since it stood inland, less exposed to the prying eyes of watchers like Mr. Perrera, who were permanently stationed all round the bay from La Linea to Algeciras. Accordingly, the furniture-vans were diverted via Falasco's house, where their loads were completed.

"Our various bits of equipment—respirators, rubber suits, oxygen bottles etc.—reached us hidden inside the furniture. Two large bottles of compressed air, which were too big to travel this way, were dressed up in hats and coats and brought home at night on the back seat of the Peugeot. They looked like two people drunk or half asleep and fortunately no one was sufficiently inquisitive to ask who they were. The problem of bringing in the limpet-mines was more serious. They could hardly go in the furniture and for some time we could not think of any way of fetching them from Falasco's. Finally, we solved the problem by hiding them in sacks of coal, which we ordered, of course, through Falasco. It was, perhaps, rather a large quantity for a small villa with only two people in it; but no one bothered to investigate."

The various equipments were assembled at the Villa; and this was not so easy as it may sound. It was essential, for one thing, to avoid arousing the suspicions of the Spanish daily-woman and not to leave about any identifiable debris, such as boxes, wax paper, rubber bags, empty bottles or unused explosives.

"We threw everything down the well behind the house at night, when no one could see us. It was a deep, unused well. After the operation on the night of 12th July, I also threw down some limpets which had not been used. They exploded about a couple of months later; but everyone thought it was a bomb dropped from an aircraft which was aiming at Gibraltar.

"The operation on the 12th was the first to start from the villa. That day there was a *fiesta* at La Linea, which drew a crowd of people from neighbouring villages. We decided to take advantage of this to bring across to the villa the swimmers who had meanwhile arrived on *Olterra*. That evening, Conchita and I went to La Linea and danced where everyone could see us. Then we came straight home to get the operation ready . . . I had decided to take part myself, but received orders from Falasco to stay behind, as he considered my presence more necessary on shore."

In this operation—Borghese puts it on the night of the 13th not the 12th—twelve frogmen took part: two officers, two petty officers, two divers and six ratings or leading-seamen. They left the villa after dark and made their way along the dry bed of a stream, whose wooded banks gave them cover for the few yards to the sea. They were, in fact, unobserved except by some dogs who started barking—fairly enough considering what was going on under their noses. But all was well; no alarm was given to whoever was watching the Villa Carmela. The twelve frogmen had a clear road to their objective, the merchantmen of a large convoy which was then in Gibraltar harbour.

That night the S.S. *Shuma, Baron Douglas, Meta* and *Empire Snipe* all blew up. That they were not all a total loss was only due to the speed with which the British managed to beach them. All four ships were put out of the war for the duration. In fact, a total of ten ships had been mined; but the premature explosion of one limpet gave the alarm and the waters of the harbour were searched, the ships minutely examined and many of the charges removed. But not all. . . .

After this operation all our men got back safely to Spain. Some reached the Villa Carmela; others were arrested on the beach by *carabineros*, but released after the intervention of the Italian consul in Algeciras.

The odd thing is that the British did not realise at the time that the attack came from Spain. They thought that the saboteurs had been dispatched from a submarine in the harbour as had happened a few months before at Alexandria and in the previous year at Gibraltar itself. Their destroyers and corvettes put out to sea at once to search for this imaginary boat. But in the end they must have known or guessed the truth, because a triple barbed-wire fence, decorated with chevaux-de-frise and other obstacles, was run out along the foreshore between Gibraltar and Algeciras. Mr. Perrera and his minions also began to bivouac permanently round the Villa

Carmela—presumably not with the idea of serenading Conchita.

But it needed more than barbed-wire or troops of Perreras to stop the Villa. On the night of 15th September the frogmen were in action again. Only three ships were at anchor outside the naval basin and three swimmers accordingly went out: Lieut. Straulino and Leading-Seamen Di Lorenzo and Giari.

"Everything was organised as before, but we had one new and unforeseen difficulty to overcome. Mr. Perrera was still on watch; but it had nothing to do with him. It took the form of an unexpected visit by General Molino, the Governor of Algeciras, his brother, who commanded the Naval Base, and their wives. I never discovered whether the visit was simply an unusual example of Spanish courtesy or whether some particular motive lay behind it. However, there they were. They arrived at the Villa during the afternoon and stayed until late in the evening, while we were expecting the swimmers and had a thousand and one things to see to. And the house, as you can suppose, was upside down. . . ."

I can imagine the scene. The frogmen's limpets in one corner; diving-suits and aqualungs piled here and there; waterproof cases and bottles of oxygen all over the place; a forgotten box in the most conspicuous position; and, in the middle of the mêlée, Conchita giving her guests tea and chatting brightly about her uncle in Madrid. All this for hours, while everyone was waiting for Straulino, Di Lorenzo and Giari to arrive, as, in fact, they did a quarter of an hour after the guests had left at nine o'clock.

This time the operation was less successful, as only one ship, *Raven's Point*, was sunk. But by September the

British had taken to berthing their ships directly opposite the naval basin, if not inside it, and to posting watchmen on board, who periodically threw explosive charges into the water. Consequently, to sink even one ship out of the three present was not bad work, especially when you remember that only three swimmers were employed, all of whom returned safely.

So ended the story of the Villa Carmela, a less romantic story than some people have made out, but for that very reason better worth the telling.

CHAPTER XIV

## THE GHOST SHIPS

UCH HAS been written, both in England and Italy, about the Battle of Cape Matapan. We know every last detail of that unhappy affair. We know the circumstances which led to the disastrous night-action; the courses of all the ships engaged; the positions of the British battleships and cruisers; the speed of the enemy destroyers which chased the damaged *Vittorio Veneto*, but failed to catch her; the movements of Admiral Cattaneo's cruisers, *Zara* and *Fiume*, which were both lost; and how it was that *Pola* came to find herself torpedoed and stationary in mid-ocean. In short, we know everything, both from Admiral Iachino's account and from the detailed analysis of the battle in Admiral Bernotti's history of the war. There would be no point in saying anything more, were it not for certain well-authenticated phenomena which occurred during the battle and of which mere common-sense can provide no explanation.

Not long ago, for example, a bottle was washed ashore containing a dying message from one of the ratings killed in the action off Matapan. The bottle was found on a beach in Sardinia. Inside was a paper bearing the words: "Signori, tell my Mother I am dying for my country. Thank-you, signori, thank-you." The writer was Francesco Chirico, a seaman from Futani; and his message was scribbled as his ship, the *Fiume,* was sinking. At the last moment he thought of something else and added after his name the words, "Italia, Italia." They expressed all that he felt, but did not know how to say, as his ship went down. He committed his message to the sea, and the sea faithfully delivered it eleven years later.

I have no wish to comment on this message from eternity. You will say that it was pure chance that a jettisoned bottle, adrift in the Mediterranean for eleven years, should find its way at last to an Italian beach. So it was. But it was a chance which fits exactly into the pattern of strange events surrounding Matapan. Some people may be able to find a prosaic explanation; but I cannot.

A great many things about the battle can be explained. We know, for example, why the British did not open fire at once after spotting the *Pola* by radar, but turned away in search of other ships, which might not have been there at all. We can understand how the course of our two cruisers came to coincide with that of the British 15-inch battleships and why it was that the British, well served by the planes from their aircraft-carrier, knew exactly which Italian ships were at sea, whereas we had only a general idea that Cunningham's battle fleet was out. All this, as I say, can be explained. What remains entirely inexplicable is why seamen on both sides—the British without exception and many Italians as well—saw during the action a light cruiser of the *Colleoni* class, which was not in fact there at all.

There is no need to give an account of the whole engagement. It is enough to recall that on the night of 28th March, the cruiser *Pola,* badly hit by an air-torpedo, was stationary, and that the heavy cruisers *Zara* and

*Fiume*, with four destroyers under Admiral Cattaneo, had been sent to her aid. The cruisers were steaming in line ahead, *Zara* leading, followed by the destroyers. They were the only Italian ships moving in the area, *Pola*, though not far off, being still stationary. Yet all the British accounts maintain that ahead of *Zara*, the flagship, was a light cruiser of the *Colleoni* class. It was so reported at the time; and Admiral Cunningham has told the same story in his recent memoirs. There is thus no room for doubt that the British officers and men concerned did actually see this non-existent ship.

The precise time at which she was first picked up is given: 2228 hours. She was a light cruiser of the *Colleoni* class and was sailing ahead of *Zara*, like an outrider to the Italian formation. It is also stated that she was fired on and that fires were started on board, which forced her to break off the action.

*Zara* and *Fiume*, as we know, not being equipped with radar, were taken by surprise and were both sunk before they could fire a shot. *Pola*, a silent and inactive spectator of the fight, was also sunk. But what of the light cruiser? No ship of that class took part in the engagement at any stage, either that night off Cape Matapan or earlier in the day off Gavdo Island. Her appearance was a myth or the result of mass-hallucination. But can any illusion of that sort be strong enough to persuade a captain and his crew to open fire on a ship which isn't there; or an admiral to report afterwards that the ship in question caught fire?

If it was an illusion, it was a strange one; and it is made all the stranger by the fact that, eight months before, the *Bartolomeo Colleoni* herself had been sunk in those very waters by the Australian cruiser *Sydney*. The *Colleoni* can scarcely have been present at Matapan in person; but her ghost was certainly there, drawing the enemy's fire. The enemy saw her, and she was also seen from the deck of the helpless *Pola*. But no one could do much for the Italian ships that night, not even a visible but non-existent light cruiser.

But the strangest story which that sad night-action produced, is another one. Admiral Iachino mentions it in his *Gaudo e Matapan* and so do other writers. I was told it by a seaman from Naples who was with me in the Red Sea and in the Atlantic in *Torelli* and was afterwards posted to *Fiume*. All that I can remember about him is that his name was Antonio. When he came to see me on *Da Recco*, he told me, with tears in his eyes, the story of *Fiume's* loss. The first salvo had taken her by surprise. Her Captain, Giorgio Giorgis, had tried in vain to bring the resulting fires under control, and had finally given the order to abandon ship. He himself had stayed on board; and they had seen him in the stern lighting a cigarette as he made his way forward to the bridge for the last time.

The survivors were adrift on rafts and in boats for five days. They suffered a good deal; but it was not that which left its mark on Antonio, so much as a sight which they all saw at dawn on the second day:

"There was nothing in sight, only flat, oily sea. So we all saw her plain enough when she began to come up, four or five miles away. First the crow's nest, then the mast and funnels. We couldn't help but know her. It was our own ship, *Fiume*, coming back for us. We could see her bridge and her gun-turrets. She heaved herself out of the water till her decks were almost awash, but so slowly that we thought she was dying. We thought she had come to fetch us, because some of us were pretty far gone by then. But she stayed where she was without ever seeming to shake quite free of the water. Then, very slowly, she began to sink again and that was that."

That was the story that Antonio told me more than a year later. Perhaps I ought to have spoken to him about mirages and the power of suggestion. But who was I to destroy his belief that his ship had made a dying effort to rescue her crew? Besides, I am still convinced that *Fiume* did come back with a message for those who would listen, the same message that she sent last year by the hand of Francesco Chirico of Futani.

# THE CONVOY BATTLE

## CHAPTER XV

## AFRICAN CONVOYS

### I

THE long-drawn-out convoy battle in the central Mediterranean was the most desperate and bitter engagement fought by the Italian Navy during the war. It was made the more so by the fact that the enemy's strength, equipment and tactical skill improved month by month, almost day by day, whereas our ships, our weapons and even our tactical methods remained much the same throughout. As time went on, it became clearer and clearer that we could never win. But the prospect of defeat did not daunt our seamen or shake their resolve to keep the Army supplied with what it needed. Their courage showed, if anything, more brightly in 1943 than in 1940 or 1941, though by then it was obvious to everyone that the battle had been lost irretrievably.

Let me try to describe the conditions of the struggle. It was made up of a series of sea and air actions fought over or around our convoys in the central Mediterranean. These actions, though extended over a period of more than three years, all had a common objective and can, therefore, properly be regarded as a single battle. It was a battle in which there were no pauses or intervals of rest. Every single day between June 1940 and March 1943 saw an action somewhere between the British and our Libyan or later Tunisian convoys. The unrelenting nature of the struggle has often been forgotten, though it was the first of the two main factors which shaped the course of events.

The second was the limited area within which the whole battle had to be fought. Few people have paused to consider that our convoy routes were necessarily restricted to the narrow waters between Southern Italy and the African coast. Convoys had to leave from ports in South Italy, if they were to reach Tripoli and Benghazi; and this gave them little room for manœuvre or evasive routeing. Their course lay, willy-nilly, within the quadrilateral formed by the Narrows and the Straits of Otranto in the north and the two ports of discharge in the south. And later, when we had lost Benghazi, the quadrilateral narrowed to a triangle. No matter how ingenious we tried to be, this was our beat, whether we liked it or not. And plumb in the middle of the area was the agreeable island of Malta, which the enemy maintained throughout the war as an offensive base for aircraft, submarines and surface forces.

A couple of radar-equipped aircraft[1] flying over the area for two or three hours could fix the position of all the ships at sea between Italy and N. Africa. Once that had been done, enemy aircraft or cruisers could be directed onto the convoy or patrolling submarines manœuvred into position for an attack. Nothing could have been simpler, for the low speed of our merchantmen made it difficult for them to take evasive action once they had

[1] The range of the enemy's radar was between thirty and sixty miles.

been spotted. It was a matter of target-practice by night, for the British, knowing that we were not equipped with radar, usually preferred to wait for darkness. No one doubts the fighting quality of the British; but in the last war they showed a remarkable predilection for actions in which they could see and we could not.

To make the position clearer, let me tabulate these four main points:

1. Our convoys were tied down to the narrow stretch of water between their ports of arrival and departure.

2. In the centre of this area was a well-equipped enemy base, which was in effective action throughout the war.

3. At least one convoy—and often more than one—had to pass through this threatened zone every day.

4. Radar-equipped aircraft from Malta had no difficulty in picking up our convoys, especially since they knew that something was bound to be there.

It followed that every convoy was subject to continuous attack throughout the whole of its two, three or four days' voyage. A convoy from Taranto to Benghazi, for example, usually suffered its first attack from submarines patrolling off the Italian coast. It was then picked up by radar in the Ionian Sea and hammered for the entire night by bombers and torpedo-carrying aircraft. These were usually joined by submarines patrolling in the approaches to Benghazi and directed to the scene of action from the air. To all this had often to be added the operations of cruisers and destroyers from Malta. Finally, there were further attacks by enemy aircraft and submarines off the African coast.

Our escort vessels fought back with great vigour, so that every voyage was a continuous running battle. This lasted with some changes of tempo but without any real interval, day after day for three years. Nevertheless, during that period, out of 2,500,000 tons of oil and dry cargo despatched, 1,900,000 were safely landed at Libyan ports. The total loss en route was approximately 14 per cent, oil included. This was certainly a high rate of loss but not the crippling one which is generally supposed. I must add, moreover, that ninety per cent of all the troops carried were landed safely.

These figures refer only to the Libyan route. Losses in convoys to Tunisia, as we shall see, were higher. On the other hand, the Albanian, Greek and Ægean convoys had a much lower rate of loss. Though I shall not say anything about these latter routes, it would be wrong to assume that they were entirely unmolested. Even in the Adriatic, and still more in the Ægean, Italian merchant ships had to sail in convoy and escorted. A number of furious battles between ships, aircraft and submarines took place in these seas as elsewhere, with only this difference—that we got the better of it. For this credit must be given both to the organisers of the convoys and to the seamen who plied between Brindisi, Durazzo, Valona, Corinth, Rhodes and the Piraeus. Their work was so effective that one can say—broadly speaking—that everything reached its destination without loss.

(I hope that my friend Barbini will forgive me if I pass over his heroic defence with *Fabrizi* of the convoy which he was escorting from Valona to Brindisi on the night of 12th November 1940.)

II

I must now make one point clear. Our Mediterranean convoys bore little resemblance to the huge, heavily escorted merchant fleets of twenty, thirty, seventy or even a hundred ships which come naturally to mind when one speaks of convoys. In one sense, of course, this picture is correct, for the term "convoy" implies the gathering together of a large fleet, and that was the method used by the Allies in the Atlantic. But our Mediterranean convoys were differently organised, partly because the sea-route was so short, and partly because of the limited berthing capacity of the Libyan ports. It would have been useless as well as dangerous to have brought in more ships at any one time than could be unloaded. Now in 1941 and 1942, so far as I remember, Tripoli could only handle five or six ships at a time and Benghazi only three of four. Conditions in Tobruk varied very greatly; but the maximum was not more than three or four ships.

It followed that our convoys had to consist of a very small number of ships, evenly matched in speed and with an adequate escort. The largest convoy even to put to sea (whether you reckon in numbers of ships or total tonnage) consisted of eleven merchantmen. The important but ill-fated *Duisburg* convoy, of which more hereafter, contained seven ships. Among the six-ship convoys I may, perhaps, be allowed to recall one, which had *Da Recco* as her chief escort and reached Tripoli intact on 12th May 1942. The unloading produced such a congestion of vehicles, petrol and munitions on the dockside that an air-raid would have been a real disaster.

But even six- or seven-ship convoys were exceptional; convoys often consisted of no more than two ships and two escorts; and there were many—convoys in name only —which comprised only single ships with an escort of one or at most two old torpedo boats. For example, the transatlantic liners *Esperia* and *Victoria* reached Tripoli on 25th June 1940, escorted by the two torpedo boats *Orsa* and *Procione*. The ships *Ankara* and *Monviso* came into Benghazi in the summer of 1942 under the escort of *Da Recco* and *Saetta*. The tanker *Lago Tana*, sailing independently and unescorted, reached Tobruk safely in September 1942, during one of the worst periods of all. The list could be extended indefinitely; and I have only quoted these examples to show how dangerous it is to generalise. Some convoys reached port safely with small escorts or none at all; others, though heavily escorted, were destroyed or dispersed.

I should like to avoid encumbering these pages with statistics; but something must be said, not only of total losses, but also of their various causes. I therefore give below a short table, prepared by the Naval Historical Section, which shows the number and total tonnage of all Italian merchantmen lost between 15th June 1940 and 8th September 1943, analysed by cause:

| Cause of Loss | Number of Ships | Gross Tonnage |
|---|---|---|
| Submarine | 324 | 810,093 |
| Air attack in port | 364 | 378,058 |
| Air attack at sea | 125 | 396,181 |
| Surface ships | 59 | 122,791 |
| Other causes | 452 | 399,398 |
| Total | 1,324 | 2,106,521 |

Over a thousand ships, representing more than two million gross tons—perhaps even more if all losses were counted. It is a very high figure indeed, which few people could have foreseen at the beginning of the war. Could we have done better? That is a question which one is bound to ask; and the answer, on an impartial view, is "yes", provided that sufficient thought had been given in peacetime to two problems. The first or strategic problem was the capture of Malta; the second or material one, the provision in good time of enough escort vessels and the training of their crews. But both these problems, though correctly appreciated, were left unsolved.

It is true that the Admiralty made a careful study before the war of sea communications between Italy and North Africa. But the result was wholly negative, the planners reaching the conclusion that, in a war against England and France combined, the problem would be insoluble. This assertion was contained in one of the memoranda which the Chiefs of Staff put up periodically to the Head of the Government. I do not know what reaction it aroused; but in naval circles there was certainly a keen appreciation of our probable difficulty in supplying the Army in North Africa. Indeed, in the paper already quoted, it was stated in plain terms that if we persisted in the attempt we should end by losing our entire Navy and merchant fleet.

The possibility of reducing Malta was examined in an attached staff study; but, so far as I can discover, the project never went very far. Nor did the plans for providing an adequate number of escort ships. The reason, no doubt, was the same in both cases. Since the authorities had already decided that it would be impossible to keep open our sea communications with Libya, there was obviously no point in knocking one's head against the wall in a vain search for an answer.

Once the war had started, and especially after the fall of France, the situation changed. It was seen that something could, after all, be done and had to be done. If heavy losses were accepted, at least a limited flow of supplies could be guaranteed. This was the start of our central Mediterranean convoys, which plied continuously for the next three years between Naples, Taranto or Brindisi and Tripoli, Benghazi or Tobruk.

We have seen that the two liners *Esperia* and *Victoria* arrived in Tripoli in June 1940 with an escort of only two torpedo boats. I should add that, while the convoy system was being worked out, the Army was supplied by submarines, by old torpedo boats and by the 1st and 11th Destroyer Divisions. Of all these operations, only that carried out by the 1st Division was unsuccessful.

On this occasion our ships, having been spotted by reconnaissance planes from Malta, were intercepted by a British cruiser squadron, which had no difficulty in sinking the flotilla leader *Espero*. That she was the only casualty was due to the gallantry of her commander, Captain Enrico Baroni, who sacrificed himself and his ship to save the rest of his force.

This was the first clash between British and Italian surface forces, and it was a clear demonstration of the dangers of the Libyan route. Accordingly, the next convoy of five motor ships, which left Naples on 6th July, was escorted initially by a cruiser squadron as well as light craft. Then, when the Admiralty learnt from the submarine *Beilul* that the enemy's main fleet from Alexandria was at sea and heading for the central Mediterranean, more cruisers and the battleships *Cesare* and *Cavour* were added to the escort. The convoy reached its destination safely, though the escort had to fight an action on the way off the Calabrian coast. The action had no results either strategic or tactical but ended creditably for our ships, which stood up well to an attack by three battleships and the aircraft carrier *Eagle* led by Admiral Cunningham in person.

III

It will be seen from the table given above that the heaviest losses were those inflicted by submarines; they were about double the losses by air attack and five times as great as those from surface forces. It was these last which made the most stir at the time; but they had comparatively little effect on the flow of supplies to Libya. The really serious threat was from the enemy's submarine offensive. This would have been a great deal easier to meet had we been able to escort our convoys with anti-submarine corvettes, with aircraft carriers and with long-range aircraft, on the system which enabled the Allies to get the better of the U-boat offensive in the Atlantic. The same methods would have been very useful in the Mediterranean; but they depended on careful preparation in peacetime.

As it was, we found ourselves at the outbreak of war short of escort vessels and without suitable long-range aircraft. As for aircraft carriers they did not exist even on paper. We could not, therefore, give our convoys complete protection against submarines and suffered painful losses in consequence, such as the two big motor ships *Oceania* and *Neptunia*, which were sunk in a single action by the submarine *Upholder* on 8th December 1941. The two ships had left Taranto on 17th September with an escort of five destroyers and were sailing in company with *Vulcania* when they were both hit by the same salvo of torpedoes from *Upholder*, who had penetrated the destroyer screen. *Neptunia* sank about three hours later. *Oceania* might have survived, had she not been hit again by two more torpedoes, also fired by *Upholder*, which finished her. *Vulcania* succeeded in breaking contact and, despite a further attack by submarines and aircraft, reached Tripoli safely with one ship of the escort, *Usodimare*. The other four destroyers remained on the scene of action to pick up survivors and were, in fact, able to rescue 5,818 men of the 6,000 troops carried by *Oceania* and *Neptunia*.

Let me add here a few more names of ships sunk by submarine attack in 1941 and 1942:

S.S. *Conte Rosso* and *Esperia*, transatlantic liners, on 24.5.41 ten miles off Augusta, and on 20.8.41 eleven miles off Tripoli; both in waters where protection should have been possible, if the necessary anti-submarine craft had existed.

S.S. *Palma* and *Valdivagna* on 9.1.41 off Cape Carbonara; *Martinolich* on the same day at Bova Marina. *Cita di Messina* on 15.1.41 off Homs. *Ursus* on 31.1.41 between Lissa and Cursola. *Juventus* on 16.2.41 off Tunis. *Colomba La Faro* and *Merzameni* on 5.3.41 off Capo delle Armi. *Fenicia* on 10.3.41. *Carnia* on 23.3.41 in the Adriatic. *Ticino* and *Laura Corrado* on 26.3.41 and 30.3.41 north of Trapani. *Fianona* on 12.6.41 off Leghorn. *Isarco* on 5.9.41. *Providenza*, tanker, on 22.9.41 off Ischia. *Veniero* on 9.12.41 south of Navarino, homeward bound with British P.O.W.s on board. *Del Greco* and *Filzi* on 13.12.41 south of Taranto. *Galitea* on 29.3.42 in the Ægean. *Delia* off Brindisi. *Camperio*, by a submarine later sunk by the escort *Da Recco*. *Enrichetta* on 10.10.42 south of Navarino. *Castelverde* and *Honestas* on 15.12.42. *Emma, Edda, Utilitas, Foscarini*. . . .

I have no wish to continue the list. These names are enough to show what the submarine offensive meant to our convoys. It is true, of course, that for every successful attack there were at least two or three that failed. It is also true that our losses did not always go unavenged, as witness the forty British submarines which were sunk in the Mediterranean. But neither fact is much consolation beside the 324 large Italian merchantmen sent to the bottom by British or Allied submarines.

IV

I said above that it was the offensive by surface ships which received the most publicity, especially after the attack on the *Duisburg* convoy on the night of 9th November 1941. There is no need to describe this action in detail, since much has been written about it already. It is enough to recall that this convoy of seven ships, escorted by the cruisers *Trieste* and *Trento* with eleven destroyers, was attacked by the cruisers *Aurora* and *Penelope* and the destroyers *Lance* and *Lively* and wiped out in a few minutes. If the British attack had occurred in daylight, the result might well have been different; but at night radar gave the British an immense superiority. I need not repeat that these night actions between ships with and without radar resembled duels between a blind man and one who could see. It would have been a strange thing indeed, if victory on the 9th November had gone to the blind. It should also be noted that, whereas the British inflicted very heavy losses on us by night, as at Cape Matapan and the action off Kerkennah[1] or on 9th November 1941 and 2nd December 1942,[2] they had little or no success by day. The most that they ever achieved —in the actions off Calabria, Cape Spartivento, Gavdo

[1] See Chapter XVII.
[2] When British light forces sank four ships of a Tunis-bound convoy and two escorting destroyers. (Tr.)

Island, in the Gulf of Sirte or off Pantelleria—was "nothing neither way".

In the case of the *Duisburg* convoy (comprising five Italian and two German ships) the British force left Malta after nightfall, relying on radar to guide them to their target, and made a surprise attack from the dark side of the horizon. A British account of the action remarks among other things that "seventeen minutes passed between the moment of sighting and the firing of the first shot". During this long interval our ships saw nothing of the enemy, who were able to take up their positions at leisure. Then, as soon as the order to fire was given, the convoy was destroyed in a few minutes; and the British ships disengaged immediately before our two cruisers could be brought into action. The destroyer *Fulmine*, which returned the enemy's fire, was sunk, and her two consorts, *Grecale* and *Euro*, which also moved in to the attack, were seriously damaged. This is not the place for a critical examination of an action which was little more than a piece of target practice by night; but it will be clear that the tactical advantage conferred by radar made the enemy's victory inevitable.

In other night attacks the enemy's surface forces sank five ships of the *Tarigo* and three ships of the *Da Recco* convoys; but the grand total in three years of war was no more than fifty-nine ships of approximately 123,000 tons. An examination of all the evidence, including that of the various actions which ended in our favour, leads to the conclusion that the threat from enemy surface ships was the one the Admiralty best understood and was best able to deal with. They never hesitated to take the whole fleet to sea, when there was reason to suppose that Cunningham's battle squadron was out or that a striking force was operating from Malta. Nor did they hesitate to use cruisers or battleships as escorts when it was necessary. In December 1941, for example, a convoy of only four ships for Tripoli and Benghazi was escorted by three battleships, including the *Littorio*, two cruiser squadrons and twenty destroyers. The result was the first battle of Sirte.[1] The action off Calabria in July 1940 also originated in an escort operation carried out by the whole fleet.

To sum up: it will be clear from what has been said and from the figures quoted that the defence of our convoys against surface attack proved not unsatisfactory, despite the observations of certain Italian and foreign commentators, who have written from hearsay, from prejudice or even from malice. Of course, it would have been folly to have used cruisers or battleships as escorts on occasions when there was no threat of surface attack. The consumption of fuel was prohibitive and, in any case, cruisers and battleships are no protection against submarines or air attack. To have sent out the main fleet when there was no chance of its meeting an equivalent British force would have been a serious blunder; and it was to the Admiralty's credit that they did not make it.

## V

Fighters are the only effective defence against air attack; but, though we had good pilots and machines, our available force was far too small for the multitudinous offensive and defensive tasks which needed to be carried out

---

[1] On 17th December 1941 three cruisers and fourteen destroyers under Rear-Admiral Vian encountered two Italian battleships and various light forces to the north-west of Benghazi. When Admiral Vian attacked, the Italian ships drew away to the north. The two forces were only in contact for about an hour. (Tr.)

in the Mediterranean. As a result, convoys were sometimes escorted by very few aircraft or only over a short section of their route. Some had no air escort at all or only two or three JU88's, which were no match for the enemy's four-engined aircraft.

In the early part of the war British bombers and torpedo bombers could only operate at a limited range from their bases in Malta or Egypt and our losses at sea were proportionately small. During 1940 our main losses—mostly of ships of small tonnage—came from the bombing of ports; and it was not until the spring of 1941 that air attack at sea became a serious problem. But it rapidly reached such proportions that our losses in the second half of that year were the worst of the whole war.

It was also during this period that the R.A.F. began to develop the technique of night attacks. Convoys were spotted by radar-equipped aircraft and flares were then dropped to light up the scene for the bombers and torpedo bombers. The crews of the ships under attack had no warning, for the noise of the ships' engines drowned the drone of the aircraft; and they had no radar or air escort. Their only defence, when the flares came down, was to lay smoke and zigzag in an attempt to disturb the enemy's aim.

These attacks, lasting for four or five hours or even for the whole night, put a severe strain on the morale of the crews, who had the unpleasant feeling of being at the enemy's mercy. Flares lit up the scene like daylight; bombs fell; and they could see the torpedo tracks in the water. Perhaps a lull followed; but the crews knew that "they" were still up there, waiting for a favourable opportunity or a gap in the protecting smoke. The next bomb might fall that moment, next day or next month. Yet

An armed merchant ship seen through the periscope of a submarine.

A U.S. convoy en route to Italy passes an Italian submarine bound for Malta.

The Italian destroyer *Da Recco*, hit in a night engagement while escorting a convoy in the Sicilian Channel, is assisted by ships sent out from Trapani.

The Italian submarine *Galileo Galilei* being captured by the British trawler *Moonstone*.

the crews kept at it throughout the war, without rest and without slackening the rhythm of the shuttle service beween Italy, Tunis and Libya.

Who of those who went through it will ever forget those interminable night hours under constant attack from an invisible enemy?

In homage to those who were lost, I give below the names of some of the larger ships sunk by the R.A.F. in 1941:

*Po,* a hospital ship; S.S. *Mazzini* and *Urania,* in the Red Sea; *Montello; Beatrice C.,* in the Gulf of Gabes; *Nita, Adua* and *Maddalena Odero;* M.V. *Andrea Gritti,* a very painful loss; S.S. *Caffaro* and *Nicolo Odero, Rialto, Cassaregis* and *Bainsizza; Caterina, Achille, Capo Faro* and *Perla.* . . . These are only a few of the names; but they are those which will, perhaps, be most familiar to the seamen of Italy.

The heavy air attacks on Malta, which began early in 1942, quickly reduced our rate of loss. In May and June the total losses by air attack, including losses in port, amounted to only 50,000 tons. But from August onwards, as the attack on Malta slackened, the situation again deteriorated. From then on it grew steadily worse as the range of the enemy aircraft increased, their radar equipment improved and the U.S.A.A.F. also began to take a hand. By May 1943 losses by air action alone had risen to 80,000 tons in a single month, the highest figure of the whole war.

It only remains to add more names to the sad list of ships sunk by air attack:

M.V. *Victoria* on 24.1.42, the loveliest ship in our merchant fleet, torpedoed with 1,400 troops on board, of whom 1,060 were saved; M.V. *Allegri* at dawn on 31.5.42, carrying munitions; she exploded and all but three of her crew were killed; *Giuliani* and *Vettor Pisani*; S.S. *Arno* shortly after midnight on 9.9.42, a hospital ship, illuminated and showing her markings clearly; *Proserpina, Sanandrea, Saturno, Giuliani,* tankers; M.V. *Zara, Brioni, Foscolo, Caucaso,* etc. . . .

The British, of course, attacked our ships in port as well as at sea; and we lost many while they were loading or unloading or waiting in harbour between trips. This explains the apparent discrepancy between the number of ships sunk and the relatively small percentage of cargo lost. I remember especially the blowing up of the two ammunition ships *Prospero* and *Citta di Bari* in Benghazi and Tripoli respectively, which seriously damaged a number of ships berthed nearby and caused the loss of the torpedo boat *Canopo*; also the sinking, again in Tripoli, of the tanker *Panuco* and two cargo boats and, most unjustifiably, of the hospital ship *Virgilio* just as she was about to leave harbour. Another hospital ship, *California,* was sunk in Augusta harbour by torpedo bombers.

When merchant-ship losses rose to an alarming point, the Admiralty fell back on submarines and light naval craft for the transport of oil and stores to Libya. In 1941 submarines carried more than 4,000 tons of oil or dry cargo, and other supplies were carried by the cruiser *Cadorna*. But this misuse of warships was inevitably costly. The submarines *Saint Bon, Atropo* and *Caracciol* and the cruisers *Diaz, Da Barbiano* and *Da Giussano* were all lost in this way, in addition to the smaller ships sunk in the ordinary course of escort duty.

To complete the roll of honour I ought now to add some of the names of the little ships—the sloops, fishing boats, tugs, auxiliary schooners and other small craft—

which were used in coastal traffic or even on the run
between Sicily and Libya. Many of these gallant boats
were lost, either in passage or at their moorings in ill-
defended harbours. But what is the use of giving names
—the lugger *San Basilio* sunk on 9th June 1941; the auxiliary schooner *Filuccio* set on fire by a burning aircraft
off Zuara; the brigantines *Usai, Paolina, Lillebeo* and
*Numziata* with six other sailing ships bombed in Cag-
liari harbour by American Flying Fortresses on 28th
February 1943? These names mean little by themselves;
they are only part of the tragic story implicit in the figures
already quoted: 1,324 ships of a total of 2,106,521 tons
lost by enemy action.

VI

I have already quoted this round figure of two million
tons[1] more than once: one million tons lost at sea and
one million in port. But in fact Italy's total loss during
the war worked out at more than three million tons of
shipping. The discrepancy is explained by the number of
merchant ships—a total of 1,240,000 tons, to be exact—
which were caught by the outbreak of war outside the
Mediterranean and unable to return to their home ports.
Much might be written about the mentality of the then
Chief of State, who allowed our merchant ships to go
about their ordinary business in every quarter of the
globe, even after Italy's entry into the war had been
decided. As the result, some of our best, largest and
fastest ships found themselves the furthest from home.
. . . But I do not want to be drawn into a political
argument. I will only add that this mistake was not
made by England, who cancelled normal sailings in the

[1] The Allies lost more than twenty million tons of shipping during the war.

131

Mediterranean in the summer of 1939, or by Germany or even, on such a wholesale scale, by Japan. It was only Italian merchant ships that continued their usual sailings right up to the end.

On the evening of 10th June 1940 the masters of nearly a thousand ocean-going ships had to face the most difficult problem of their careers. They solved it under very varying conditions as best they could with no more than the most general instructions to guide them. Whatever solution they found—whether by scuppering, like the M.V. *Romolo* off the Solomons or the S.S. *Timavo* off Durban, or by seeking refuge in friendly or neutral ports—they all preserved their honour and that of the flag under which they sailed. Only a very small proportion of the fleet was captured—thirty-six ships in all, which had no chance to save themselves as they were actually anchored in British ports. All the remainder—that is, the vast majority of those caught outside the Mediterranean— were either scuppered or sold to neutral countries or given refuge in friendly ports in South America or the Far East.

## CHAPTER XVI

## BLOCKADE RUNNERS

ANYONE who had suggested before the war that Italian ships would be able to make successful voyages between France and Japan under the conditions prevailing from 1940 to 1943, would have been regarded as mad. In 1938 or 1939 no sane man would have predicted that Italy, while at war with both Great Britain and the United States, would still be able to allow herself the luxury of sending ordinary cargo-carrying ships halfway round the world, across the Atlantic, the Indian Ocean and the Pacific.

Nevertheless, it was done; and it was one of the most remarkable achievements of the war. The ships in question were unarmed merchantmen, sailing independently. They set out in the first place from neutral ports, where their crews had been enjoying a comfort and security which many people might have envied. But when the call came to an adventure, the hazards of which were obvious, they responded without hesitation. To do so needed courage of a particular kind—courage which for once was not measured in terms of the number of men killed. They weighed anchor and left their ports of refuge, loaded deep with goods and raw materials which were unobtainable in Axis Europe.

Three ships left from the Far East, the M.V. *Cortellazzo*, *Orseolo* and *Fusijama*. The first named sailed with

6,000 tons of cargo and an extra load of fuel in her bilge tanks. She left Korea on 16th November 1941, disguised as a Japanese, crossed the Pacific, rounded Cape Horn and sailed up the Atlantic to Bordeaux, where she arrived on 28th January 1942, seventy-two days out from Dairen, after a voyage of 21,000 miles. A chance encounter in the Pacific had forced her to make a sudden change of course; and Japan's entry into the war had involved a new disguise, improvised with some canvas and a few tins of paint. But these were her only difficulties.

*Orseolo* and *Fusijama* were equally successful. They left Kobe on 2nd December 1941 and 7th February 1942, each with about 6,000 tons of useful cargo. *Fusijama's* voyage was the more eventful of the two. She was sighted several times by enemy ships, attacked by Japanese aircraft in the Pacific and intercepted by a British aircraft in the South Atlantic. But the Japs did no harm and the Englishman, evidently a decent fellow, was satisfied with her disguise. So *Fusijama* also got home safely.

We have seen already that thirty-six of the 220 Italian ships caught outside home waters at the outbreak of war were captured by the British. Another large group, mainly of passenger ships, were interned by the United States, who returned nearly all of them at the end of the war—*Conte Grande, Conte Biancamano, Aida Lauro, Mar Glauco, Iole Fassio, Saturnia, Voluntas,* etc. Many others were able to take refuge in neutral ports or in Italian ports in the Red Sea. In 1941, these last found themselves in a very awkward position, hemmed in between the British bases at Suez and Aden and without any friendly or neutral port for which to run. There were thirty-seven of them in all, of which most were scuppered when Massawa and Assab fell to the British. *India,*

*Sannio II, Piave* and some others were all lost in this way. The *Duca degli Abruzzi* and *Somalia,* on the other hand, were able to reach Diego Suarez, though they too were sunk in the end, when the British captured that port. The M.V. *Himalaya* had a much happier fate. After a daring passage through the Perim Straits, she managed to escape the enemy's search and reached Brazil on 3rd April 1941, after a voyage as bold as it was uneventful. She did not linger in Brazil but left again shortly with a cargo of hides and metal and arrived in Bordeaux on 30th April 1941.

Other ships from the Red Sea, including *Ramb I, Ramb II* and *Eritrea,* made for the Far East.[1] Both *Ramb II* and *Eritrea* reached eastern ports safely, though only after a number of unwelcome encounters, from which they escaped by skilful navigation and an adroit use of smoke. While crossing the Malay Archipelago, *Eritrea* (Commander Iannucci) had to take on Portuguese nationality—a disguise effected, as usual, by a lavish use of paint, some canvas, a little timber, and, of course, a Portuguese flag. The result was apparently good enough to deceive the Dutch aircraft, which circled her several times, trying to make out her identity. At any rate, they allowed her to pass.

Luck, on the other hand, ran against *Ramb I* (Commander Fiorelli) and led her straight into the arms of the cruiser *Leander* in the Indian Ocean. She tried the ruse of running up English colours but was ordered to heave-to. *Ramb I* then hoisted her own colours and opened fire with her two guns. The battle lasted about an hour; but gun duels between cruisers and merchant-

[1] Technically, *Eritrea* was a warship, but her speed was so low and her armament so light that she counted as a merchantman for all practical purposes.

men can only end one way. Nevertheless, great honour is due to Commander Fiorelli, who was posthumously awarded the Gold Cross, and her crew for their gallant resistance to an immeasurably superior enemy.

The problem confronting our ships in South American ports was less difficult—though still far from easy—since they had no narrow waters to pass. But, in fact, only a few of them chose to face the risks of an Atlantic crossing. The majority were sold instead to various South American states, though a few were restored to Italy after the war. I must add, however, that between March and July 1941, four ships—*Frisco, Mombaldo, XXIV Maggio* and *Africana*—reached France from Brazil with valuable cargoes. Other ships, also in burthen, came into Bordeaux or St. Nazaire from Las Palmas, Tenerife or ports in Spain, and the tanker *Fidelitas* from Scandinavia.

All these ships, of course, had to sail alone and unescorted and some of them were lost on the way. The S.S. *Caboto*, for example, scuppered herself in the Persian Gulf to avoid capture; *Ernani* and *Recco* were torpedoed by submarines; *Sangro* fell a victim to an auxiliary cruiser; *Butterfly* was sunk by gunfire off the French coast; and the tanker *Franco Martelli*, with oil from Brazil, was sunk by a submarine just outside St. Nazaire. Most of the crew of this last ship were picked up by a German E-boat and I saw them as they came ashore. They were all suffering from the oil they had swallowed in the water, but still more from the bitterness of having lost their ship on the last lap of their 9,000-mile voyage.

This gradual accumulation of Italian ships at Bordeaux set the politicians and the Naval Staff wondering whether they could not be used to keep open trade with Japan. If ordinary cargo boats had run the blockade once, might they not succeed a second and third time? It was an attractive idea, not only because the trade would be useful, but also for the propaganda value of an operation which would demonstrate that the high seas were not, after all, entirely closed to the Axis.

After much debate it was decided to try the experiment of running Italian ships to Japan with mercury, crated aircraft and machine tools on the outward voyage and cotton and rubber on the return voyage. Four ships, the M.V. *Himalaya*, which reached France from the Red Sea and Brazil, *Cortellazzo*, *Fusijama* and *Orseolo* were selected. In the end *Fusijama* was unable to leave. *Cortellazzo* cleared from Bordeaux on 29th November 1942, but was attacked by a cruiser and destroyers off the Azores and had to scupper herself. The *Himalaya* ran into a heavy air attack in the Bay of Biscay and was forced back. The M.V. *Orseolo* (Lieut. Tarchiana), however, succeeded in making the double trip across the Atlantic and the Indian Ocean. She left Bordeaux on 1st October 1942 for Singapore by the Cape route. She reached her destination on 2nd December 1942, after a number of adventures, including the sighting of more than one enemy ship, which she avoided by a miracle, and a brush in the China Sea with an American submarine which, however, put herself so close alongside that she was unable to use her armament.

*Orseolo* left the Far East again on 25th January 1943, with a cargo of rubber and about twenty German soldiers as passengers. She came back by the same route, again sighted enemy ships and again avoided them. The climax came when she was entering the Bay of Biscay and had already picked up her German escort. A patrolling submarine fired three torpedoes at her. She was able to dodge two; but the third blew a great rent in her stern. But *Orseolo* was a tough ship and managed to reach port under her own steam.

The best tribute that one can pay *Orseolo* is to put down the bare figures: 163 days at sea, 54,000 miles covered in waters patrolled day and night by the enemy. With the exception of four German wireless operators, all her crew were Italian.

## CHAPTER XVII

## A DRAMA IN TWO ACTS

THE setting of this story is the Narrows, the strip of water between Sicily and North Africa, which no Italian sailor can now pass without uncovering. The story itself is in two sharply contrasted scenes; the first a moonlight scene made lurid by explosions, gunflashes and star shells; the second, a silent, almost furtive scene which only the most attentive observer would have noticed at all.

The first scene was during one of the many clashes between Italian convoys and British cruisers and destroyers. It took place on the night of 16th April 1941, close under the Kerkennah banks in the Gulf of Gabes; and it ended, like so many similar night actions, with the destruction of the convoy.

On this occasion the convoy and its escort were under the command of Commander Piero De Cristoforo, in *Tarigo*. He had no resemblance at all to the conventional tough hero of films and thrillers, being, on the contrary, fair, slightly built and gentle-mannered. His character matched his appearance; he was a retiring man with the diffident manner which comes from a careful upbringing. Yet at the crisis of his life as a seaman and a fighting man he showed what an indomitable spirit was hidden behind this shy exterior, which seemed so much more charming than vigorous. But it appeared when the time came that De Cristoforo had in fact the heart of a hero, coupled with a fortitude which still seems barely credible. The answer lay in his deep, almost mystical patriotism.

His career before the war had been much the same as anyone else's. He had served afloat and in campaigns overseas and had had one posting in the Far East. He had also held the appointment (which usually went to a naval lieutenant) of A.D.C. to H.R.H. the Prince of Piedmont—an honour which he owed as much to his personal and social as to his professional gifts. On his promotion he had to leave the Court at Naples; and the outbreak of war found him Captain of the *Tarigo* with the rank of Commander. She was one of twelve destroyers of the *Navigatori* class which, being old and not very fast, were used for all kinds of jobs and especially for the dangerous and responsible work of escorting African convoys. You may judge what this meant from the fact that of these twelve ships only one, my own *Da Recco*, was still afloat at the Armistice.

De Cristoforo might well have claimed a better posting —to a flotilla-leader for example. But he was not the type of man either to wangle anything or to complain. He accepted *Tarigo* as what fate and the Admiralty had given him and took up his duties forthwith.

We must now come back to the early hours of 17th April. A calm night with a little moon showing; five cargo boats sailing under the lee of Kerkennah, escorted by *Tarigo* with the destroyers *Lampo* and *Baleno* in company. At two in the morning they were only a few hours' steaming from Tripoli; but this was the most dangerous part of the route, within easy range of Malta, whence British cruisers and destroyers were then operating. And Malta was alert, for a reconnaissance plane had spotted the convoy shortly before midnight. Our ships knew nothing of this; nor was there any action they could have taken if they had done.

The attack developed about two o'clock, the British force coming in from astern on the dark side of the horizon, invisible to our ships, who were clearly silhouetted against the moon. It was a well-planned surprise, delivered at the right moment and from the most favourable angle. How many British ships were there? I do not know exactly[1]—a cruiser or two, certainly, and a number of destroyers, helped out—in the usual British whirlwind technique—by fighters and aircraft dropping flares.

*Tarigo* was hit at once by a salvo which exploded her magazine and tore her bridge apart. De Cristoforo had his leg blown off, but, as soon as a tourniquet had been applied, he insisted on carrying on and directing operations. *Baleno* and *Lampo* were also hit before they even knew what was happening. All *Baleno's* officers were killed, including her Captain. *Lampo* managed to fire a few rounds from her guns and five torpedoes before, riddled with shot, she ran aground on the Kerkennah reefs. It was all over in a few minutes, or perhaps seconds.

*Tarigo*, with her commander mortally injured, continued the action at great odds—an old and damaged destroyer against uninjured cruisers and destroyers, supported by aircraft. But De Cristoforo wanted at all costs to keep the British force engaged so that the remaining ships of the convoy could make good their escape. (One of them, the *Arta*, was in fact able to beach herself.) The odds were now one against five or six and the outcome not difficult to foresee.

[1] Actually, the four destroyers of the 14th Flotilla (Capt. P. J. Mack). (Tr.)

It was a heroic fight, for *Tarigo* was drawing the enemy's whole fire. Several officers were killed and casualties among the crew were heavy; but De Cristoforo, with extraordinary determination, kept his ship in action and her remaining 4.7-inch guns firing. The main magazine had already gone; there was a fire in the stokehold; and *Tarigo*, now no more than a smoking ruin, was hove to. Luca Balzofiore, her engineer officer, blinded by the flash of an explosion, had himself led up to the bridge to make his last report to the Captain and to die with him.

When the last gun had fallen silent De Cristoforo was still able to summon enough strength to direct the firing of the remaining torpedoes. His orders were carried out by Sub.-Lt. Besagno—hardly more than a boy—who was still miraculously unhurt. He behaved with the greatest steadiness and was able to score a direct hit on H.M.S. *Mohawk* and sink her.

That was *Tarigo's* last act of defiance; but one thing remained for her Captain, to see to the safety of his ship. He roused out the survivors of his crew to fight the fires, which had now taken serious hold; and they all set to, wounded and uninjured together, among the tangle of dismounted guns, red-hot metal and wrecked machinery. But the end had come. *Tarigo* turned over and sank, her colours flying and her dying Captain at his post. The British ships drew off; and the survivors of *Tarigo*, *Lampo*, *Baleno* and *Mohawk* and of the cargo boats *Sabaudia*, *Adana*, *Aegina*, *Arta* and *Isernia* were left in the water to be picked up next morning by the hospital ship *Orlando*.

We now come to the second act, which began in a closely guarded room in the Admiralty and ended at sea. The leading character is a scruffy, smelly trawler such as can be seen on any part of the sea or in any port in war as much as in peacetime; a most innocent, unwarlike boat, at least in appearance. But all kinds of mysterious jobs came the way of trawlers during the war and even before it, when some countries used them for espionage.

This particular boat snorted and smoked her way to the scene of the action of 17th April. Her ostensible purpose was to fish; and the place she selected, curiously enough, was exactly over the spot, discovered after patient search, where *Mohawk* had gone down. She placed herself so that no watcher on shore could see what she was doing, and then quietly slipped a diver overboard. He remained below far longer than was necessary to clear the screw or free a net from the bottom. . . . The trawler stayed in the same position for three days, keeping up a pretence of fishing, while the diver rummaged *Mohawk's* hull. At last a line drew up a curious, perforated steel box. It was full of books, which were more precious than the richest treasure trove because they contained the *Mohawk's*—and therefore the Royal Navy's—confidential papers, ciphers and signal procedure. Intelligence officers in a trawler, equipped for a rather specialised kind of fishing, had carried out to perfection the plan hatched in the Admiralty.

The papers in the steel box had been thoroughly soaked by sea water and their jackets spoiled; but no one minded about that. They still contained invaluable information which enabled us to decipher British naval signals for many months to come. But eventually the inmates of the corresponding room in the Admiralty in London began to notice that the Italians knew altogether too much. Then it was our turn to start again from the beginning —and so on throughout the war.

## *DA MOSTO'S* LAST FIGHT

THE DESTROYER *Da Mosto* kept up her fire against the British cruisers *Aurora* and *Penelope* until the 4.7-inch guns on her forecastle were awash. Her stern had been blown off by the explosion of the after-magazine and her decks were under water. She could no longer move or steer; and it was only a question of time before she sank. Yet she continued to fight so long as her forward guns were above water: two 4.7-inch guns against the twelve 6-inch of the cruisers and the five 4.7's of their escorting destroyer.

Francesco Dell'Anno, *Da Mosto's* captain, and his crew were fighters of the kind who do not count the cost. They took the view that a battle went on as long as any weapon could be brought to bear or men were still alive to work it. So *Da Mosto* kept her colours flying to the end, when she was no more than a jagged lump of metal, sticking out of the water like a half-tide rock. When she finally sank, her three opponents lined their decks and steamed slowly over the spot in a last tribute to the old ship, which had fought so desperately to protect the convoy in her charge.

The word convoy is perhaps misleading in this connection, for *Da Mosto* had only one ship, the tanker *Mantovani*, under her wing. But, as I pointed out above, this arrangement was not uncommon. The action on 1st

December, 1941, was not the only occasion when a tanker
ran the Narrows with only a single destroyer as escort.
Some critics may express surprise at a policy which could
send out ships so lightly escorted in broad daylight within
a few miles of Malta, which was then in full operation as
an offensive base. I offer no comment on this, apart from
what has already been said in an earlier chapter. I can
only repeat that the battle of the convoys was the
bloodiest and most desperate engagement fought by the
Italian Navy during the war.

*Da Mosto* and *Mantovani* were about seventy miles
from Tripoli at 1300 hours when the inevitable attack by
torpedo bombers burst upon them. *Mantovani* was hit at
once and brought to a standstill. But, though unable to
move, she was still afloat; and it was still possible—though
at great risk—to take her in tow, bring her into port and
salvage her cargo. Dell'Anno, after a rapid review of the
position, decided to try. At the second attempt he succeeded in getting a line on board—a difficult manœuvre
duly recognised in the subsequent citation: "The merchant ship in his charge having been hit and put out of
action, he attempted with great professional skill, while
under heavy air attack, to take her in tow. . . ." This bald
account does less than justice to the occasion. While the
aircraft straddled her with bombs and torpedoes *Da
Mosto* tried to save what could be saved without any
regard for her own safety, and fought back as best as she
could with her quickfirers and her main armament. This
strange duel between bombers and a destroyer trying to
salvage a tanker, went on for some hours and might even
have ended in *Da Mosto's* favour, if *Aurora*, *Penelope*
and an enemy destroyer had not appeared on the scene
at about 1800 hours.

"0558 hours: Explosion observed on board the third destroyer of the enemy formation.

0559 hours: Range 7,000 yards to merchantmen; 6,000 to destroyers. First torpedo salvo fired. Gunfire directed alternately on destroyer and merchantmen, when later visible through the smoke screen."

A routine report containing no more detail than is needed to convey the facts. But that laconic style was typical of Castrogiovanni, one of the ten or twelve captains who commanded destroyer flotillas during the war. It found its final expression six months later, on 17th December 1942, when he was lost with his latest command, *Aviere*, when she was torpedoed and broken in two by a British submarine. But Castrogiovanni had always had the same vein of austerity even as a young midshipman in 1916, when he found himself in the water after the sinking of the destroyer *Nembo*, but clung to his raft and refused to be rescued by an enemy ship. This incident was commemorated on a gold medal, which the city of Florence wished to present to him and for which D'Annunzio composed the inscription: "We will never truckle to death or the enemy."

Castrogiovanni's approach to life was always the same, whether in the Adriatic in 1916, on convoy duty in the Mediterranean in 1941 and 1942, in the action of Pantelleria or in the Narrows where he met his death.

But let us come back to his log. It records the hits obtained on another destroyer and a merchantman by *Vivaldi* and *Malocello*; then comes this passage:

"0620 hours: A shell explodes in the forward engine-room. Steam and oil pipes perforated by splinters. Other shell fragments start fire in adjacent main magazine...."

148

At a range of five or six thousand yards—analogous to a pistol duel in Nelson's day—it was inevitable that the Italian ships should be hit sooner or later. What is surprising is that it was only *Vivaldi* that suffered and only to the extent of a single shot. But she was now stationary, with a serious fire on board, within close range of the enemy ships, and under heavy attack from their guns and torpedoes. Nevertheless, she kept up her own rate of fire, even though her main turret had to be operated by hand. When the British destroyer *H68* came so close that the name on her stern could be read, *Vivaldi* fired two torpedoes and forced her to withdraw.

*Malocello* remained alongside *Vivaldi*. The description of the action in a recent and much-discussed book contains the sentence: "Only two destroyers, *Vivaldi* and *Malocello*, tried to approach the convoy during the English destroyers' attack; but one of them, having received a hit in her engine-room, was immobilised and the other retired." May the writer be forgiven for these closing words. *Malocello* did not retire, but stayed with her damaged consort, laid a protective smoke screen and defended her with guns, torpedoes and quickfirers against the British destroyers and the aircraft which presently arrived from Malta. Castrogiovanni's log continues in its blunt style:

"0645 hours: *Malocello* circles *Vivaldi*, lays smoke and puts up a heavy barrage."

Shortly after seven o'clock the British abandoned their prize and drew off. But there still remains another enemy, the fire below, which threatened *Vivaldi* increasingly for many hours to come. It did not begin to slacken until the afternoon and was not finally brought under control until about ten o'clock that night. The fire crept forward from the engine-room towards the centre of the ship, caused explosions in No. 2 magazine, reached the forward gun turret and spread thence to the ammunition lockers for the quickfirers and finally to the oil tanks, from which jets of burning fuel ran along the waterways and over the deck.

But *Vivaldi* did not give up. Castrogiovanni remained calmly at his post, almost in the centre of the flames. He asked *Malocello* to send over further supplies of fire-fighting equipment and to take his most serious casualties on board. But the fire was now too fierce to be controlled by any apparatus on *Malocello*, even with the help of *Premuda*, *Oriani* and *Ascari* who had now come up. It was essential to bring *Vivaldi* into Pantelleria, where the equipment at the naval base could be used to smother the flames. But this could not be done until late that evening, though according to Castrogiovanni's log it was still only nine in the morning. They had another twelve hours of fire-fighting before them while explosions took place in the magazine and the enemy from time to time renewed their attack:

"0936 hours: Four Swordfish torpedo bombers attack *Vivaldi* and *Malocello*, both hove to, at a range of sixty yards.

0950 hours: A formation of seven bombers over the two ships which reply with intense A.A. fire. A near miss by stick of about thirty bombs on the port quarter."

The burning ship was not taken in tow by *Premuda* until 1020 hours. Then began the slow and difficult trip to Pantelleria, where Castrogiovanni hoped, even if he could not dock his ship, to beach her and prevent her loss. It is at this point that we find the only entry in his log which is not strictly official:

"1028 hours: The crew is making untiring efforts to control the fire, regardless of flames and explosions. I am proud of them."

After this one sentence the log takes up its prosaic tale again, with no further mention of the captain's feelings, which can still move us, intense as they must have been. I had always been a friend of Castrogiovanni's and his keen admirer, and felt it deeply when I heard of his death in the same waters in which *Da Recco* had endured so much only a few days before. But it was not until I read the minute-by-minute account in his log that I understood the full measure of his unassuming courage.

The tow to Pantelleria proceeded. The wounded were taken off in hospital boats sent from the naval base and most of *Vivaldi's* crew put ashore. Only the officers, petty-officers and about fifty able seamen remained on board—and, of course, the captain. *Premuda* had the tow and *Malocello* stood by to render help, if necessary. *Ascari* and *Oriani* had both rejoined the 7th division.

*Vivaldi* was saved; but she left Pantelleria for Trapani and later Taranto in such a condition that many months were needed to repair her. In fact, the re-fit lasted for nearly a year and had hardly been completed before she was sunk on 9th September 1943, in action against the Germans off the Straits of Bonifacio.

Castrogiovanni was not a man to stay idle for a whole year. He asked for the command of another flotilla-leader and was given *Aviera*. He returned to the escort of Medi-

terranean convoys, a service in which he acquitted himself
so well that, during his whole tour of duty for the summer
of 1941 to the end of 1942, no merchant ship and no
escort vessel was lost under his command. He escorted
dozens of convoys from Italy to North Africa and back
again and at various times used his own ship to run
urgently needed petrol to Tobruk or ammunition to
Benghazi. He was ambushed by submarines, tracked by
radar, lit up by flares and attacked by bombers and torpedo bombers, but emerged triumphantly from it all.
This was a distinction which he shared with Galati, who
commanded the *Vivaldi* flotilla from 1940 to the summer
of 1941, and which he kept until his last voyage on 17th
December 1942.

Even on that occasion the M.V. *Ankara* and the
destroyer *Camicia Nera* reached Biserta safely, though
*Aviere,* the flagship, was hit by two torpedoes from a
patrolling submarine in what was later known to both
sides as "death alley", where twenty-one escorts were sunk
in three months, to say nothing of submarines, E-boats
and merchant ships. The enemy attack developed about
11 a.m. Perhaps Castrogiovanni put his ship bodily across
the track of torpedoes aimed at the *Ankara*; at any rate,
she was hit at once and sank in a few seconds, blown in
two, with her bows pointing skyward.

A hundred men or so, the captain among them, found
themselves in the water, probably with no clear idea of
how they got there. They assembled round a few pieces
of floating debris and two Carley floats—big rafts, with
ratlines round them, supported by metal buoyancy tanks.
The attacking submarine had, of course, disappeared.
*Ankara* and *Camicia Nera*, who might have lingered
(especially the latter) to pick up survivors, had both with-

drawn as fast as possible from what was evidently a danger zone. Nothing remained for the men in the water but their bits of wreckage, the two Carleys and the immense moral support of their captain. "He was calm and imperturbable," said the survivors, "with a word of encouragement for everyone; he said that we would soon be getting our own back."

The men had to struggle against rough seas, the poisonous oil in which they were floating, the cold and the biting wind. Castrogiovanni did not only encourage his men but made the only sacrifice left him and gave up his place on the Carley to a seaman whose strength was failing. When the torpedo boats *Calliope* and *Perseo* reached the scene that afternoon, he had disappeared, "completing," in the words of the citation, "by an act of sacrifice a life entirely devoted to his country and his Service."

## CHAPTER XX

## COMMANDER ENEA PICCHIO

ON HIS arrival at Taranto after a long tour of duty escorting Mediterranean convoys in the summer of 1942, *Saetta's* skipper, Commander Enea Picchio, reported to the captain commanding the escort group and said, smiling:

"You know, sir, during this last trip you never gave me any orders or made any signals."

There was no formality about making one's report after these difficult wartime trips. The destroyers and torpedoboats came into their moorings in succession; and their skippers gathered on the quay to discuss their experiences and express their views, pretty freely, about the Admiralty and shore-based authorities in general. These meetings often took place at night after a late return from a trip which might have lasted four or five days on end. Everyone felt the need to talk even more strongly than the universal need for sleep or a drink. It was a necessary release of nervous tension.

There was no formality even when there were noticeable differences of age or rank. We were all living the same life and running the same risks; and almost all of us were inspired by the same enthusiasm. So our official reports turned into conversations and a profitable exchange of ideas, while they were still fresh in our minds.

The Captain's reply to Picchio was: "Why should I give orders or make signals when you do what's necessary off your own bat?"

They talked for a little longer about their trip—three merchant ships brought safely from Benghazi to Taranto through a succession of air attacks. They agreed that the best plan was always to open fire on aircraft as soon as they were spotted, even at night and even if there was no chance of hitting them. Then they went back to their ships, Picchio as pleased with the Captain's comment as if he had been decorated or patted on the back by the Admiralty.

He was a quiet, self-contained man; a good officer, who took the war in the Mediterranean seriously but without fuss. As a Lieutenant he had commanded the torpedo-boat *Andromeda* when she was engaged in the arduous duty of escorting convoys from Brindisi to Valona or Durazzo at the time of the Italian attack on Greece. He had then been put in charge of the island of Saseno, a more difficult and complicated job than it may sound but certainly not one to satisfy a man like Picchio whose ambition was a roving commission in the Mediterranean, the more dangerous the better. On 9th July 1941, he wrote to his sister: "What annoys me most is to be slaving away in a shore job. . . . I'm wearing myself out here and it's driving me nuts. The pen is not (repeat not) my weapon, so I am going to apply for a ship."

His application went forward and was accepted at the beginning of 1942, when he was given command of *Saetta*. She was a small, old and slow destroyer, of the type normally used for escort duty, which the Admiralty fondly believed could be carried out by less efficient ships than those assigned to service with the Fleet. But Picchio, now a Lt.-Commander, knew exactly what he was letting himself in for and welcomed it—a job which was responsible, dangerous and exhausting, but essential to the war-effort.

Picchio began his service on the North African run, plying between Brindisi or Taranto and Benghazi, Tripoli or, later, Tobruk, when that port had been recaptured. It was a wearing life, for each convoy, crawling at the speed of its slowest ship, had to fight its way through, and there was no rest even in port with Benghazi and Tobruk under incessant attack by the R.A.F. *Saetta* sailed sometimes as a unit of the escort, sometimes in command and always showed herself equal to the task, whether it was using her meagre armament against the enemy, picking up survivors or acting as a screen for the merchantmen.

There was no doubt of Picchio's success. When *Saetta* had completed her 100th trip, the Commander-in-Chief, Admiral Iachino, paid her a visit at Taranto to congratulate her captain and crew. But the work went on just the same. Next day *Saetta* sailed again, this time not on convoy duty, but with the task of towing to Benghazi or Tobruk an old submarine of the *Balilla* class, loaded with petrol and oil. These were curious trips, about which not much has been written, but fully as dangerous as any other and requiring a high standard of seamanship. Ocean-going submarines no longer fit for operations were stripped down to the bare hull, their engines, armament and gear being taken out, and were used as lighters for the transport of fuel. They had two advantages over conventional craft of this kind: they could be towed at a higher speed (fourteen instead of four or five knots); and they were almost invisible on the surface.

In the middle of August 1942, *Saetta* had just reached Benghazi on one of these towing operations, when she received orders to join a convoy sailing for Italy. It consisted of the M.V. *Bixio* and *Sestriere*, *Da Recco* commanding the escort and the torpedo-boats *Orione* and *Castore*. It was a good convoy, fast and well-matched. But neither the speed nor the efficiency of the escort saved *Bixio* from receiving two torpedo-hits from a submarine off Navarino. This area was one of the worst in the Mediterranean; one could always be certain of finding an enemy submarine lying in wait there. This time, judging from the number of torpedo-tracks, there must have been more than one. *Da Recco* laid a pattern of depth-charges round *Bixio* and would then have given certain orders to the rest of the escort. But there was no need. *Castore* had already taken *Sestriere* in charge and was hurrying her away from the danger-zone; *Saetta* had laid herself alongside *Bixio* and managed with great skill to pass a tow-line.

*Bixio* was at least ten times larger than the destroyer; she had been holed by the torpedoes and was making water, so that she was unnaturally heavy and sluggish. Yet Picchio managed to get his tow working, bad weather and the constant danger of submarines notwithstanding. He took the damaged ship into Navarino and, though the distance was only twenty miles, it needed the whole night—about ten hours—to do it.

From Navarino, Picchio wrote to his mother: "A lot of compliments have been flying round the last few days. There has even been talk of putting me in for the Silver Cross. All God's doing; but I think I can say that I did my best, too." The turn of phrase was entirely characteristic—a true reflection of the spirit which upheld him.

of the Service. Having given orders to abandon ship and satisfied himself that no one was still on board, he returned to the bridge, unwilling to desert *Saetta* in which he had served so long. The men in the boats saw him salute the colours as she went down.

Such was the death of one whom his fellow-officers described as "one of the ablest, bravest and most dashing destroyer-captains that Italy ever had."

PART IV

FOUR BRAVE MEN

CHAPTER XXI

ADMIRAL CARLO BERGAMINI

N o one will ever know what happened in the control-tower of the *Roma* on the afternoon of 9th September, 1943, when the German air-attack burst on her, because all the persons present, from Admiral Bergamini downwards, were lost with the ship. Only one thing is certain: that the Admiral had no thoughts for himself, for his distant family or for anything but the ships and men under his command.

Perhaps Bergamini, with his great faith in naval gunnery and the strength of the 35,000-ton battleships, which were in a sense his own creation, never even considered the possibility that one or two bombs from an aircraft might destroy these enormous ships. Even if he did, it was certainly not his own fate which preoccupied him. The last message from the flagship was a faint wireless-signal: "We are in danger," and then, after a pause, "mortal danger." But these words, sent immediately before the final explosion, were not dictated by the Admiral, who would never have authorised a cry for help in such faltering terms. His own last word was the flag

F

signal ordering a change of formation, which *Roma* was still flying when she went down, as if in evidence of the Admiral's intense determination to do whatever was possible for the safety of his fleet.

Carlo Bergamini was outstanding among his countrymen for his gifts of leadership. He was also a man of great technical knowledge who left his mark on the new Fleet, which was built up almost from scratch between the wars. (His work on gunnery-development was eagerly followed in France and England.) But his greatest and best remembered attribute was his deep humanity, which the responsibilities of high command never smothered or weakened. As Admiral Iachino says of him: "He was a modest, unflamboyant man, though not without ordinary professional ambition, calm in times of stress and naturally magnanimous, with no malice or venom and a great sympathy for human weakness. . . . He had a strong hold on the affections of the lower deck. His men looked on him as a father and would have followed him anywhere.[1]

I remember him when he was in command of the cruiser *Bande Nere* during the Abyssinian war. He seldom went ashore, but spent each evening in port seeing anyone who asked for an interview, whether for advice in some difficulty or simply to spend a few moments with him. They were all his sons—petty-officers or young seamen; and it was always as a father that he led them. Even as Commander-in-Chief, he never dealt with officers or men as entries on a nominal roll, but invariably as human beings, men or boys whom he knew and whose strengths and weaknesses he understood. He had the same feeling for his ships, which he loved like living creatures

[1] V. Angelo Jachino: *Le due Sirti.*

and cherished, not only in their paint and brasswork, but as fighting units, able to protect those who sailed in them. He spent much more time afloat than in shore-going technical or administrative posts. Any crisis was sure to find him at sea, as he was during the Abyssinian war or again during the whole period from 1940 to 1943. At the outbreak of the late war he was in command of the battle-squadron which included the two 35,000 tonners, *Littorio* and *Vittoroi Veneto*, both newly commissioned. (No one was better qualified than Bergamini to bring these ships, the Navy's main strength, to a state of fighting efficiency.) At the time of the action off Calabria he wanted to take them to sea, though they were not yet fully worked up, and offer battle to Cunningham, who was then standing in boldly for the Ionian Sea. The most stringent orders from the Admiralty were needed to veto this plan. In the circumstances these orders were prudent and sensible; whether they were wise is another matter. A seemingly reckless decision sometimes decides the issue of a battle or even a war; and it may well be that the whole course of future events would have been different if, on 9th July, 1940, Cunningham had been caught between the fires of Campioni's squadron and Bergamini's capital ships, even though the latter were not yet fully efficient.

At the beginning of 1941, Bergamini, who had been appointed second-in-command to Admiral Iachino, was flying his flag in *Duilio*. In her he carried out a series of convoy-operations at great risk, for the old battleship when serving as an escort made a sitting (and much sought after) target for submarines and aircraft. But, so far as I remember, no ship was lost on any of these operations. This was partly the result of an effective defence, based on *Duilio's* heavy armament, and partly on Bergamini's capacity for inspiring the officers and men under his command—perhaps even the ships themselves.

Nevertheless, Bergamini missed his chance of the major engagement which would have made his name. He carried out a number of difficult operations with unvarying success; but they never brought him into action with the enemy's main fleet, even after he had succeeded Iachino as Commander-in-Chief. It was almost as if Providence had denied him a battle in order to preserve him for the hardest and most painful task of all—that of carrying out the terms of the Armistice.

He knew very little about the matter beforehand. Although he was the head of an efficient Fighting Service, no one bothered to tell him about General Castellano's mission[1] or to give him any information—still less consult him—about the Navy's intended role in the Armistice. The first that he heard of it was on 7th September at a Commanding Officers' meeting at the Admiralty, when the Minister, De Courten, without being able to say very much, threw out some hint about the result of the talks at Cassibile between the British and Italian Governments. After the meeting Bergamini returned to Spezia, to resume his command on the *Roma*. The news that the Armistice was to become effective from 8th September reached him by telephone, as did the skeleton orders which were all, in the chaos of the time, that he ever received.

Bergamini had trained the Fleet for battle, not for an Armistice or a voyage of surrender to Malta. His reaction, when he heard the news, must have been appall-

[1]General Castellano was the Italian representative in the secret negotiations with Allied Force Headquarters, which preceded the Armistice. (Tr.)

ing; but he had the strength of mind to master it. He assembled his Admirals and subordinate commanders and addressed them—and through them their ship's companies—at two meetings on board *Roma*, the first on the afternoon of the 8th, the second at about ten o'clock that night. At both meetings—more especially the evening one—he told them what he knew of the course of events. He said that the Armistice provided for the transfer of the whole Italian Fleet to a port controlled by the Allies, but that they would not be required to haul down their flags. He added that no ship should be allowed to fall into the hands of any other Power; if there were no other means of preventing it, they should be scuppered. He then said a few words, spoken from a full heart, about the dark hour through which Italy was now passing, and finished by saying that he had reached a verbal agreement with the Admiralty that for the moment the Fleet should proceed, not to an enemy port, but to La Maddalena[1], there to await further orders.

Bergamini spoke at once as a leader and the father of his men, as an officer acting under orders and, above all, as a great Italian, who knew how to put into clear and vigorous language what his hearers already felt in their hearts. His eyes were glistening as he spoke and his hands, usually so restless, were quiet.

On the night of 8th September all ships ready for sea left harbour under the Admiral's command, in good order and with their lights blacked-out, as they had so often done when going into action. There sailed from Spezia: the battleships *Roma*, wearing Admiral Bergamini's flag, *Italia* (ex *Littorio*) and *Vittorio Veneto*; the cruisers *Eugenio di Savoia* (Admiral Oliva), *Montecuccoli*

[1] The fleet-anchorage in the extreme north of Sardinia. (Tr.)

165

and *Regolo*; the destroyers *Legionario, Velite, Mitra-gliere, Oriani, Artigliere, Grecale, Fuciliere, Carabiniere, Da Noli, Vivaldi*; and a few torpedo boats. From Genoa sailed the cruisers *Garibaldi* (Admiral Biancheri), *Duca degli Abruzzi* and *Duca di Aosta*.

Only badly damaged ships, such as *Gorizia* and *Bolzano*, or ships under repair remained at Spezia. All the rest set a course to take them west of Corsica and Sardinia; all, that is, except the two destroyers *Da Noli* and *Vivaldi*. They were under orders for Civitavecchia on a mission of which little has been said but which, had it succeeded, might yet have changed the history of those troubled days.

The plan, evolved by De Courten, was for *Da Noli* and *Vivaldi* to carry the King and the Government across to Sardinia, so that the island, fortified by their presence and that of the Fleet, might continue to exert an influence on Italy's destinies. The plan, opposed by the Allies, was in any case forestalled by a German occupation of La Maddalena in the early hours of 9th September. The two destroyers, after the loss of the *Roma*, altered course for the Straits of Bonifacio to pick up survivors from the flagship.

During the night of the 8th the ships from Spezia and Genoa joined company and the whole fleet, in line ahead, having rounded Cape Corse, steered for Cape Testa (on the northern point of Sardinia) with the intention of entering La Maddalena from the west. But at about three o'clock in the afternoon, just when this change of course had been completed, a signal from Rome informed Berga-mini that German troops were already on the island. The stage was thus set for the last act of the drama. The port for which he was making being closed to him, the

Admiral altered course again to seaward. But what was to follow? We have no evidence from which to judge Bergamini's intentions. He may have planned to make for some other Italian port, though there was none in the central Mediterranean which could accommodate the whole fleet, or to head for Bône towards the British ships. But perhaps he never came to a final decision, for events overtook him suddenly and tragically, as soon as he had altered course.

At that very moment, shortly after three o'clock, a formation of five Junkers 77 was sighted, heading for the three battleships. This striking-force, armed with guided missiles of a new type,[1] pressed their attack with great determination. All the AA guns in the Fleet replied; and Bergamini ordered an immediate change of formation to confuse the enemy and disturb his aim. Nevertheless, *Italia* was hit, though not very seriously, and *Roma* was hit twice, once in the boiler-room and once between her forward 15-inch turret and the bridge.

An ordinary bomb would probably have been stopped by the protective armour after penetrating the upper and main decks; but this special missile passed straight through into the bowels of the ship and exploded in the magazine. The rest of the fleet saw *Roma's* control-tower crumple as if it had been paper and a flame as tall as a house shoot up in its place. They saw the battleship falter and then break completely in two. Both halves sank within in a matter of minutes or even seconds, after rising nearly upright in the water.

Fifteen hundred men of the *Roma's* crew went down with her and nearly all her officers, including Admiral Bergamini and his Chief of Staff, Rear-Admiral Stanislao

[1]The Fritz I, invented by Max Kramer, now in the U.S.

space was too much for him and he collapsed. The skipper would not allow him to be put in a bunk on the mess-deck, but had him moved aft to the tiny space which served as his own cabin. By doing so, he said good-bye to the two or three hours rest in the twenty-four which he had so far allowed himself; but it seemed to him only reasonable that a sick man should have such comforts as were going.

This was the normal attitude of this young Lieut.-Commander, so slight and boyish in appearance, but with a courage which few have equalled. It explains why, when *Tazzoli* had to leave on a special mission in December 1941, with only half her crew, there was almost a mutiny among those who had drawn unlucky and had to stay behind. It had nothing to do with the nature of the mission, which in any case they did not know. It was simply a protest against their skipper's monstrous act of sailing without them. They objected to being separated from him, even though missing the trip meant nothing worse than a rest, a cushy life at Bordeaux and the avoidance of a good deal of risk and discomfort.

Di Cossato had only taken command of *Tazzoli* in March, after doing a couple of patrols in her by way of apprenticeship, but he had already established that indissoluble bond with his men which was to make her a record-breaking boat. By December she had already sunk a cruiser, four cargo-boats and two tankers and had shot down a Blenheim in the mouth of the Gironde. Of these feats the most difficult had been the sinking of the tanker *Alfred Olsen,* 8,000 tons, which involved a forty-eight-hours' chase and the firing of all the remaining torpedoes —*Tazzoli* had been a month at sea—and about a hundred rounds of 4.7-inch ammunition.

In the following year *Tazzoli* had an even greater success, so that when Di Cossato finally left submarines in February 1943 he had more than 100,000 tons of enemy shipping to his credit, apart from the cruiser. But this is not the place for a detailed account of his war service. It is enough to add that, however bitterly he fought, it was always with humanity. Though he gave no quarter to merchantships, alone or in convoy, there was nothing wanton about his attacks. No shot and no torpedo was fired that was not strictly necessary; and no damaged ship was finished off until he was certain that all the crew were clear. Di Cossato always did his best to provide for survivors, even to the extent of taking the injured on board. Among others he rescued an American sergeant who, after he had been put ashore at Bordeaux, wrote a letter which is reprinted in Antonio Maronari's splendid book *Un sommergibile non è tornato alla base*: "I should like to thank the officers and men of *Tazzoli* for their kindness and attention to us while we were on board. . . . I hope Americans treat your fellows equally well. I am also writing on behalf of the others. With thanks and best wishes. John Oliver Leroy."

At the end of February 1943 the Admiralty decided that Di Cossato should leave submarines and *Tazzoli* go into dock for a long refit. Both decisions were necessary. *Tazzoli*, now known to her crew as "the old suitcase", was worn out by the many thousands of miles that she had sailed and the attacks that she had suffered from depth-charges and aircraft, while Di Cossato, after twenty-two months of continuous patrols (some lasting more than two months) in the Mediterranean and the Atlantic, was in urgent need of rest. But his ideas of what constitutes rest were evidently peculiar, for he applied at once for the command of an escort-vessel in the Mediterranean. He was given *Aliseo* and the 4th Torpedo-boat Flotilla—all new boats built during the war for escort-duty. In 1942 they had worked with the Tunisian convoys and were subsequently used, after the fall of Tunis and Bizerta, to escort German and Italian merchantmen between Italy, Corsica and Sardinia.

On 8th September 1943, Di Cossato was at Bastia with *Aliseo* and her consort *Ardito*, waiting to escort the M.V. *Humanitas* to Spezia that night. It was a perfectly normal operation, which might have ended like so many in an aircraft or submarine attack. It ended instead in a hand-to-hand fight with the Germans, which was one of the few bright episodes—the brightest of all, perhaps—in those unhappy days.

Like most other Italians, Di Cossato and his crew heard the news of the Armistice on the wireless on the afternoon of the 8th. It came as a shock to them. Having received no orders, Di Cossato recalled those men who were ashore and made ready to leave harbour with *Aliseo* and *Ardito* at midnight. *Aliseo* cast off first, following the naval custom by which the flotilla-leader is always the last in and the first away. The town was quiet and there was no reason to expect anything out of the ordinary. No one could have foretold that a few minutes later the Germans would open fire on the Italian ships, or rather on *Ardito*, for *Aliseo* was already clear of the harbour. Perhaps the Germans reacted instinctively to the news of the Armistice or were carrying out orders already received; or perhaps it was the silent departure of the torpedo-boats which gave the alarm. At all events, as *Ardito* was getting under way, she became the target of a deadly shell- and machine-gun fire from the shore-batteries and, more particularly, from the ships berthed along the quay. This unexpected fire at close range caused a number of casualties and did enough damage to force *Ardito* back to her moorings.

Di Cossato, already at sea, guessed what was happening and prepared his reply. It was probably an instinctive move rather than a carefully thought-out plan. In the Atlantic it had always been his instinct which showed him the best way to dodge the escort and sink a merchantman. So now the same impulse told him that his best chance was to stay outside the harbour and wait for dawn. He spent the night off Bastia with his gun-crews closed up at the three 4.7-inch guns and six quickfirers which made up *Aliseo's* armament. So they stood by, waiting for what he felt was bound to happen.

About 7 a.m. on 9th September the German ships—one destroyer, one gunboat and eight landing-craft—began to come out of the harbour. *Aliseo* sank them all at the cost of a few scratches. After the action, Di Cossato stayed on the scene to pick up survivors and did, in fact, pick them all up, even the obstinate ones who disdained to be rescued.

From Bastia, *Aliseo* proceeded to Portoferraio in Elba, where she arrived on the afternoon of 9th, just as all the other Italian light forces from the northern Mediterranean were coming in—torpedo-boats, corvettes, gunboats, M.T.B. Some had come of their own accord and some under orders from Admiral Aimone di Savoia Aosta or Admiral Nomis di Pollone. And, once there, they all sat down to wait, among them *Ardito*, which had followed on from Bastia after temporary repairs.

That day at Portoferraio there was much wavering and indecision. It was not provoked by the political implication of the Armistice, but solely by the fear that its terms might oblige our ships to haul down their flags. Seamen, who had never hesitated to face the enemy and had gone into battle with joy and enthusiasm, now showed a resolute refusal to accept the Armistice until they had received an official guarantee on this point. They regarded their own fate as secondary to that of the flag.

On the 10th, however, the torpedo-boats *Aliseo, Ardimentoso, Fortunale, Ariete, Indomito, Calliope* and *Animoso* left Elba for Palermo en route to Malta, but only because they had by then received direct orders from the King, supported by a statement in writing from Admiral Nomis di Pollone that "the terms of the Armistice do not include the surrender of our ships or the hauling down of the flag".[1] On these two conditions—the King's order and the Admiral's promise—they set sail for Malta. Di Cossato, now Commander, was the senior officer of the group, and it was he who urged officers and men to carry out their orders. But he also proposed that charges should be laid in the magazines, ready to explode if our ex-enemies went back on their undertaking. Later, at Malta, when the rumour went round that part of the Fleet was to be handed over to other countries, Di Cossato gave the following order to the ships of his flotilla: "If the order to hand over our ships is confirmed, wherever you may be, fire all your torpedoes and all the ammunition you have on board into the ships around you, so as to remind the Allies that promises must be respected. After that, if you are still afloat, scupper yourselves."

The spirit in which Di Cossato faced the Armistice shows clearly through these words. He obeyed orders

[1] The fourth clause in the Armistice signed on 3rd September ran: "Immediate transfer of the Italian Fleet and Italian aircraft to such points as may be designated by the Allied C.-in-C., with details of disarmament to be prescribed by him." (Tr.)

scrupulously because they were given in the King's name, and he was not a man lightly to disregard the oath of allegiance which he had taken at the age of seventeen, when he first entered the Navy. In the same spirit he carried out the escort-duties which the Allies assigned to *Aliseo*; but when an Admiral expatiated on the advantages of co-belligerency, he answered drily that he had no interest in politics and was only carrying out His Majesty's orders.

In the chaos of the ensuing months Di Cossato had only one thing to hold on to; and it was inevitable that, when a new Government was formed at Salerno in 1944, which refused the oath of loyalty to the Crown, his long-suppressed personal feelings should erupt violently. He refused to recognize the Government or carry out its orders and informed the Admiral commanding at Taranto that *Aliseo* would not sail on escort-duty the following day as ordered. Di Cossato's opinions were always clear and firmly stated. Moreover, as his English and German opponents knew, it was extremely difficult to shift him. Argument by his brother-officers and pressure from above were both equally useless once he had made up his mind. Even an interview with the Chief of the Naval Staff, who was known for his loyalty to the House of Savoy, produced no result. Di Cossato answered him as he had the others: that a Government not in allegiance to the King was unconstitutional and that its orders could not to be obeyed because they had no legal validity.

There was nothing for the Admiralty to do but dismiss him his ship and put him under close arrest for three months in the castle at Taranto. For an ordinary Commander, however brave and well-liked, the penalty would probably have been more severe. But this was Carlo di

Cossato, the idol of his men, who had no intention of allowing their Flotilla-Captain, their leader *par excellence,* to be put on the beach or punished. The whole town was in an uproar. Slogans supporting Di Cossato appeared on walls and even on the steps of the house where the Minister of Marine was staying; and naïve plans were made to rescue him by force from the castle.

As the result he was released, having been dismissed the Service, and went to Naples to stay with a friend. Outwardly he was calm and composed and seemed to be looking about for some civilian job; but something had snapped in his heart. He evidently felt that the Italy for which he had fought with such legendary courage had finally disintegrated. No doubt, too, the current atmosphere of compromise and cynical time-serving disgusted him; and he began to be conscious, perhaps for the first time, of the full weight and humiliation of defeat.

On 2nd September 1944, at the age of thirty-six, he put an end to a life which had become meaningless. He left a note for the friend with whom he was staying: "Please forgive me for doing this in your house, but my own is the other side of the lines and it is not a thing which I can do with decency in the street. If anyone asks why, say that friendship, success and an income are not everything. To go on living one must have something more, which I have lost. On the brink. . . . Cossato."

CHAPTER XXIII

# HUMAN TORPEDOES

I

REFERRING to Malta's reaction to the attack by Italian
naval assault forces on the night of 25th July
1941, a British admiral wrote among other things:
" . . . the fire from the defences lasted two minutes. Then
there was silence: there was no one left to shoot at. When
dawn came the guns found two more targets and destroyed them."

Luck went so much against the Italians on that occasion,
and the disaster was so complete, that two minutes were
enough to destroy their whole force. All the pilots engaged were killed or captured and the headquarters staff
of 10th Flotilla MAS, which planned and carried out the
operation, was practically annihilated. The two force-
commanders, Moccagatta and Giobbe, Captain Falcomatà, the M.O., and the E-boat commander, Lt. Parodi,
all died that morning. Two of the pilots, Carabelli and
Pedretti, deliberately sacrificed their lives; and Lt.-Cdr.
(E) Tesei was blown up by the charge which he had laid
himself and which he had voluntarily given an instantaneous fuse.

Tesei, the inventor and perfecter of submarine assault-
craft, had been nicknamed "the angel of death", because
he regarded every operation primarily as a moral exercise.

He was a native of Marina di Campo in Elba and a born seaman; but his greatest love was for his country, to which he gave not only his keen intelligence and technical ability but his whole being. He used to say: "It is not the outcome of a particular operation or even the whole war that matters. What is needed is men who are willing to sacrifice themselves so that future generations, inspired by their example, may have the strength to conquer." These words were Tesei's profession of faith, the gospel of a man to whom war was the ultimate test of a nation's moral fibre. Elios Toschi,[1] perhaps his closest friend and intimate, writes this of him: "Tesei lives in a different world and by another scale of values—an exalted one but too sublime, too speculative. He believes that in war one must go on acting all the time, never counting the cost, never worrying about victory, because victory itself is unimportant. . . ."

War is not made, still less won, by "ifs", so it is useless to speculate what might have happened if Italy had begun hostilities with a surprise attack by a hundred or more assault-craft against British Mediterranean bases. Yet I may be allowed to dally with the idea for a moment, because this was the plan formed by Tesei in 1929, when he and Elios Toschi drew the first sketches for the human torpedo or S.L.C. I heard about the plan from a close friend of Tesei—a senior officer, much older than he was —who told me that the original designs for this ingenious and deadly weapon had been submitted in 1929, when Tesei was still an engineer-sub-lieutenant. At that time war with England did not seem even remotely probable; and the schemes of Tesei and Toschi had no precise

---

[1] *Ninth Time Lucky* is the English title of Elios Toschi's war memoirs (William Kimber, London).

objective beyond that of strengthening our naval armament. It was not until 1935 and the years following, when
the Abyssinian War had made a clash between England
and Italy inevitable, that they found their real purpose
and direction.

Tesei believed, like many other naval officers, that
Italy's limited resources and small industrial potential
gave her no chance of victory, unless she succeeded in
knocking out the British fleet by a surprise attack at
the very beginning of the war. As far back as 1935,
Tesei and Toschi had calculated that a hundred human
torpedoes, despatched to enemy bases in thirty suitably equipped submarines, and then piloted through the
boom-defences to the ships selected for mining, would be
enough to cripple the enemy's fleet for many months.
No one can say what would have happened if this project
had been carried out. Something like it was done by the
Japanese when they attacked Port Arthur in 1904 and
again at Pearl Harbour on 7th December 1941—with
startling success on both occasions. I may also quote,
perhaps, from the American naval periodical, the *O.N.I.
Review*, for January 1946: "It is the opinion of many
English officers that if the Italian Admiralty had made
unlimited use of its assault forces, specially of 'human
torpedoes', and had employed them immediately they
came into the war, the Mediterranean Fleet would have
been seriously reduced. With massive attacks at Gibraltar, Malta and Alexandria, it is possible that Italy
would immediately have gained complete control of the
Mediterranean."

179

II

Tesei's plans were originally formed, as I have said, in 1929, though only in outline. He put them forward again in greater detail in 1936, when he and Toschi had completed the design of their craft and built a proto-type, powered by the motor from an old lift. But neither then nor later was their work taken as seriously as it deserved, owing to the innate conservatism and lack of imagination, which have always been the greatest weak-ness of our Naval Staff. Between 1936 and 1940 trials, experiments and training went forward on a small scale. But Tesei and Toschi continued to improve the combined submarine and torpedo which they had invented and even built with their own hands in time snatched from their duties as engineer-officers in antiquated submarines. When war broke out they claimed the right to be first to try the new weapon against the enemy. There were many objections and difficulties, which Toschi has des-cribed in his book: "The Captain S.M. (at Spezia) was standing beside his desk talking on the telephone to Sub-marine Command in Rome. It was a long, tense con-versation: on one side a man who knew the form, could see how determined I was, and wanted to use his man-power to the best advantage; on the other a bureaucrat in difficulties who . . . didn't want to give way."

Where Tesei is concerned, we have no personal record. But his sisters have given their help in reconstructing his short life, and his brother-in-law, Engineer-Admiral Carlo Matteini, has made available a number of letters written by Tesei before the Alexandria, Gibraltar and Malta operations. In these intimate letters, full of his hopes and fears, he often quotes St. Augustine on the power of the spirit as the only means of progress.

We also owe to Admiral Matteini another incident which illustrates the self-denial that Tesei practised from the very beginning of his career. The Admiralty made an award to the inventors of the S.L.C. of a Gold Medal, First Class, for their contribution to naval science, and the sum of 15,000 lire. The two officers accepted the medal, but refused the money on the ground that a cash-value could not be given to work done purely from patriotic motives. But the Admiralty, having once allocated the money, could not take it back and the argument dragged on until the outbreak of war and after. Before he left on the Alexandria operation, Tesei arranged with Matteini to draw the money, if he did not come back, and divide it among the fitters who had worked on the project. But in fact Tesei did return after a trying ordeal and the award remained in an Admiralty suspense-account until the Under-Secretary decided to close an awkward file by expropriating it.

Tesei's first operation, carried out in the second half of August 1940, was against Alexandria. This was the first try-out of the new weapon. The pilots of the human torpedoes were Tesei, Toschi, Franzini and Birindelli, with Durand de La Penne in reserve. The approach was to be made in the submarine *Iride* under Brunetti's command from a starting-point in the little bay of Menelao in the Gulf of Bomba, not far from the Egyptian frontier. However, the operation came to a tragic end before it had really started. On 22nd August *Iride* was torpedoed by three British aircraft. She was to have left for Alexandria that evening and already had the "pigs" and some of the pilots on board. She had come out of

Penne and Birindelli, the latter being the first Italian to surmount the defences of Gibraltar and force his way into the harbour. But Tesei's trip was a perfect martyrdom.

He quitted *Sciré* about 2.30 a.m. on 30th October, but did not reach the northern entrance of the harbour until five. This was partly because his "pig" was not running well, but mainly because he had to make continual alterations of course to avoid the ships of a large convoy, which had chosen that night to sail from Gibraltar. In all it took two and a half hours' hard work, complicated by the difficulty of manœuvring his sluggish and unstable craft, by under-water charges thrown from the guard-boats, and by the congested traffic of ships and tugs. The physical strain was heavy enough to cause serious damage to Tesei's heart. But it was not this which made him abandon the operation just as he was about to reach the boom, so much as the practical question of the time-table. It was already five o'clock and too late to complete the operation before dawn. Moreover, the "pig" was no longer holding her trim and the breathing apparatus— both Tesei's and his No. 2's—was giving trouble. If they had carried on, they would certainly have been discovered and would have compromised the other pilots, of whose success nothing was then known. Tesei turned back and landed at La Linea at seven-thirty, after five hours in the water.

La Penne was also obliged to give up at the boom for much the same reasons as Tesei. Only the third pair, Birindelli and Paccagnini, managed to get into the harbour, but even they had no success because, after passing the boom, their "pig" also began to function badly. Birindelli made a spirited attempt to manhandle it under the battleship *Barham*, which was now within reach; but two hundred yards short of the target the torpedo sank for good. Birindelli and Paccagnini were taken prisoner. The other four pilots managed to get back to Italy, thanks to our excellent under-cover organisation in Spain. But Tesei's physique, already impaired by intensive under-water training and still more by his gallant rescue-work in August, never fully recovered.

In his report on the Gibraltar operation Tesei makes no mention of the gruelling hours that he spent, sub-merged or awash, in the enemy port. His account is coldly impersonal: nothing about the efforts and frustrations of the pilots, only a technical explanation of the reasons for failure. Captain Falcomatà, however, the M.O. of the 10th Flotilla, diagnosed a cardiac lesion in Tesei and declared him "unfit for underwater operations for six months". His knowledge of this weakness led Borghese later to certain conclusions about Tesei's death; but these are not supported by the facts or anything that Tesei wrote himself.

He was certainly not a man to admit that the body could prevail over the spirit; and he gave proof of this a few days after his return from Gibraltar. He was asked by the Under-Secretary at the Admiralty to apply his technical knowledge and his experience as a diver to the salvaging of the battleship *Cavour*, sunk by an air-torpedo in Taranto Harbour on 11th November 1940. This was only three or four days after the M.O. had pronounced him unfit; but as soon as he was told by Admiral Cavag-nari that his services were needed, he put on his diving-suit and spent several days investigating the wreck of the *Cavour*. The discoveries he made during a series of long dives undoubtedly contributed much to the salvaging of the ship.

## IV

To Italian seamen Malta was more than a dangerous enemy base; by implication it was a challenge. It seemed an act of historical injustice that this hostile island should exist in the middle of Mare Nostrum and on the direct route between Sicily and North Africa. Many people thought of Malta in this way; but Tesei made an attack on the island the object of his whole life. He pondered an operation against Valletta in 1935, when he and Toschi completed their designs for the human-torpedo; and his mind was still on the same subject in 1940. He continued to dream of it even when ill-health should have made him give up his work with Special Forces.

He used to say, with the conviction of one propounding a dogma, that "the world must hear of a daring attack on Malta by the Italians—the actual results are of minor importance. . . ." And, of course, as soon as G.H.Q. decided to make such an attack, he pulled every string to get himself included in the expedition, in spite of his physical condition and the fact that Moccagatta's plans, approved by the Admiralty, provided for a surface attack by *barchini* only. I must add here that this method had already been used with success at Suda Bay, where Faggioni with six *barchini*, carried by the destroyers *Sella* and *Crispi*, had sunk the cruiser *York* and about 30,000 tons of merchant shipping. It seemed logical to try the same thing again; and, in fact, the *barchini* had already made two attempts on Malta in May and June 1941. Neither had any success, but the failure, if it can be called that, had been due on one occasion to bad weather and on the other to damage to the *barchini*. The third expedition was therefore organised along the same lines.

This meant that there was no part for Tesei, the under-water expert. But having set his heart on the operation for so long, he made an urgent request—more than a request perhaps—to take part in it with his human torpedo. He encountered a certain amount of opposition at first, but had his way in the end.

I do not know whether Tesei accompanied his request with a plan for co-operation between surface and submarine craft; nor do I know what part, if any, he played in working out the plan finally used. My impression is that he did prepare an outline-plan of his own, but that it was never put into practice. But this is only guesswork, for it is notoriously difficult to reconstruct any operation after the event from the surviving records, diaries and reports. The only thing one can say for certain is that the whole affair turned out to be far more complicated than the previous operation at Suda Bay or *Sciré's* two expeditions against Gibraltar and Alexandria.

v

The assault force which sailed from Augusta on the evening of 25th July 1941 was organised as follows:

The fast tender *Diana,* with nine *barchini* on board, towing a special motor-boat on which two "pigs" were embarked.

*MAS 452* with Moccagatta, the force commander, on board.

*MAS 451,* towing a fast motor-boat, from which Lt.-Cdr. Giobbe would later direct the surface attack.

This list gives some idea of the complicated machinery which had to be set in motion that night. It was essential to the success of the operation that each move should interlock with the next according to an exact timetable. The vital point was the cutting of the net below the bridge between Fort Sant'Elmo and Valletta. It was through this gap that the *barchini* were to make their way into the harbour; and the passage had to be cleared before dawn at 4.30 a.m., because there could be no question of carrying out the surface attack by daylight.

Everything turned, therefore, on the cutting of the net; and it was natural that this job should go to Tesei in view of his known courage and experience. He was to take one of the "pigs" with Pedretti as his number two. The other, crewed by Lt. Costa and the diver Barla, was to enter Marsu Mascetto Creek independently to attack the submarines moored there. The nine *barchini* were to enter the Grand Harbour through the gap in the net blown by Tesei, having been guided as far as the entrance by Giobbe in the fast motor-boat.

Up to a certain point this plan worked well. The first hitch occurred about fifteen miles from Malta, where the MAS, the *barchini* and the two motor-boats were to part company from *Diana* and proceed independently. It was midnight when this solitary mishap took place, which would ordinarily have been of no importance, but now had the serious result of delaying the whole underwater contingent. *MAS 451*, which had taken in tow the motor-boat with the "pigs" on board, fouled her screw and collided with the tow astern. It would not have been worth mentioning but for the fact that it took the MAS more than an hour to clear the screw and get under way again. This lost hour, by delaying Tesei's attack, sealed the fate of the whole operation.

Costa, the pilot of the second "pig", who was also in charge of the motor-boat, gave this account after his release: "We were towed to within five miles of Valletta, where *MAS 451* cast off the line and stood by. At 2 a.m. I began my run in. As we had lost so much time, I approached at a much higher speed than had been planned. Nevertheless, we were able to get within 1,200 yards of the Sant'Elmo bridge without being detected. It was then about 3 a.m. We stopped and Tesei and I launched the 'pigs'. His was riding normally, but mine, probably as the result of the earlier collision, was noticeably down by the stern."

By 3 a.m., therefore, the motor-boat was within 1,200 yards of the target; but by the time the "pigs" had been launched and the trim of Costa's craft corrected, another forty-five minutes had passed. It was not until 3.45 that Tesei, now a good deal behind schedule, could start moving towards the Sant'Elmo bridge. The delay was not his fault; on the contrary, he, Costa and the other two had done everything possible to make up time. It was simply one of those hazards which always accompany an operation of this kind.

The passage under the Sant'Elmo bridge had to be cleared by 4.30 a.m. This left Tesei only three-quarters of an hour in which to reach the net, attach the warhead of the torpedo and swim clear before the explosion. It was plainly not enough. At 3.45 Tesei could still have turned back, having decided that his part in the plan was unworkable. But that would have meant the failure of the whole operation, which Tesei was not prepared even to consider. He therefore took a far more serious but highly characteristic decision. The only witness, though a good one, is Costa, who was the last person to speak to Tesei. "The plan provided," he writes, "for the blowing of the net at 4.30 precisely. . . . Tesei said: 'I don't suppose I shall be able to do more than get there in the time. But the charge will be fired at 4.30. If necessary, I shall use an instantaneous fuse.'"

That meant the almost certain sacrifice of his life; but Tesei, with his faithful companion, Alcide Pedretti, said good-bye to Costa at 3.45 a.m., having taken his decision. Borghese maintains that Tesei, knowing his state of health, "gallantly threw away what was left of his life to help his comrades and in the hope of forcing a great victory. It was done deliberately." This is only true in the sense that Tesei did decide to blow himself up. But he did not take that decision until 3.45 a.m. on the morning of 26th July, and then only because it was forced on him by circumstance. If he could have done so, he would certainly have given himself a margin of safety before the explosion. Besides, there is no evidence that he ever spoke even vaguely of suicide. The letter he wrote to Carlo Matteini, before this as before his other operations, contains no hint of any such thing. It is a moving testament of faith in his dominant idea: "Dear Carlo—A final note before the big bang. If I don't come back, please put on the funeral cards 'For King and Country—Lt.-Cdr. (E) Teseo Tesei—The Family'. Nothing more. This may sound silly, but I feel strongly about it. Please tell the Duke of Spoleto that I am going solely O.H.M.S. I don't know if we shall pull it off. 'Viva il Re! Teseo."

This is not the letter of a potential suicide. Although Tesei knew what risks he was running and faced the possibility of death, it was only in the same sense that any other member of Special Forces might have done. Another argument finally rules out any question of suicide. Tesei might have decided to end his own life; but he would never have sacrificed Alcide Pedretti's. If he involved him, it can only have been because the service required it and not by his own wish.

Tesei reached the net certainly no earlier than 4.30 a.m. and perhaps a few minutes after. He then did as he had told Costa he would do—adjusted the fuse for an instantaneous explosion. We have an account of what happened from Costa: "At about 4.45," says his report, which gives the times a few minutes late throughout, "I heard the explosion. Lt.-Cdr. Tesei had sacrificed himself. . . ."

## VI

We left the *barchini* at midnight, at the point where they parted company from *Diana*. By two o'clock they were about two miles off Malta, grouped round Giobbe's motor-boat. One of the *barchini* had been damaged and was scuppered, leaving eight, piloted by Frassetto, Carabelli, Bosio, Zaniboni, Pedrini, Folliero, Marchisio and Capriotti.

These young—very young—officers and petty-officers of the 10th Flotilla were calm and determined. Giobbe led them towards their objective to mark down the lie of the land. Twelve hundred yards from the harbour entrance, they waited for the explosion of Tesei's charge to give the signal that a passage had been opened through the net. Giobbe could not let them go until he was certain that the way was clear into the Grand Harbour. But meanwhile time was running on. It was close to dawn; streaks of light began to appear in the east and still there was no explosion. By 4.30 nothing had happened. They waited another three, four, five minutes, but they could not afford to lose any more time. Giobbe had to make up his mind either to call the operation off or to send in his men while the net was still uncut.

The men of Special Forces never gave up an operation until they had tried everything and Giobbe followed this tradition. He decided to send two *barchini* against the net and pass the remaining six into the harbour through the gap which they had made. If Tesei and Pedretti were still at or near the net, they would inevitably be blown to pieces by the explosion; but that was a risk which Giobbe had to take. It was better to lose lives than compromise the success of the operation.

Frassetto and Carabelli were ordered to blow up the net, if it were still intact. A few seconds later the rest of the party, with Bosio leading, were to pass through into the harbour. It was almost exactly at this moment that Costa, piloting his "pig" to Marsu Mascetto Creek, heard Tesei's charge explode. So did the pilots of the *barchini*; but they had received their orders, started their run, and had no choice but to carry on.

Frassetto and Carabelli headed for the net. The first, following instructions, having aimed his boat straight at the target, abandoned her about a hundred yards off. Carabelli[1] chose to remain on board, steering his frail craft to the end, so as to make certain of his target. He was killed in the subsequent explosion. On the previous evening, before the expedition sailed, he had left behind a letter for his parents: "We are going on a difficult job and the odds are against our coming back alive. I am glad of the chance to offer my life for my country and a noble cause. . . ."

Tesei and Pedretti had already given their lives, now it was Carabelli's turn. But the sad list did not stop there.

[1] Sub.-Lieut. Aristide Carabelli from Milan.

The two *barchini* of Carabelli and Frassetto went up together, almost at the same time as Tesei's torpedo. The result was a formidable explosion, much more violent than had been meant. It tore the net apart; but it also brought down one of the piers of the Sant'Elmo bridge, so that one complete span fell into the sea. The gap, for which three lives had been sacrificed, was thus effectively closed by a tangle of metal half in and half out of the water.

At the same moment all the searchlights in the base came on, converging on the six *barchini* as they headed for the Grand Harbour. Machine-guns, Bofors and Oerlikons all opened up. In the centre of this furious cross-fire the *barchini*, probably still unaware of what had happened, were dashing at full speed towards a gap which was totally obstructed. One after another they were hit and sank or caught fire. All their pilots were more or less seriously wounded. Only Bosio's boat at the head of the line was still miraculously afloat; but the rudder had jammed and she was turning in a close circle out of her pilot's control. Zaniboni, wounded and in the water, saw what was happening. He also saw that a British launch had come out of Malta in search of survivors and was heading towards Bosio. He set out laboriously to swim to the derelict *barchini* in the hope of preventing her capture and rescuing the pilot. But neither he nor the launch were in time: Bosio forestalled them both by blowing up his boat. He was the fourth Italian to sacrifice himself that day rather than fail in his duty.

Zaniboni, Frassetto, Pedrini, Folliero, Marchisio and Capriotti were taken prisoners; as also was Costa after he had destroyed his torpedo.

The reaction of the defence was too quick and the fire too well synchronised to have been the result of an unexpected alarm. As we now know, the alert had been given before either Tesei's or Carabelli's charges exploded, for the assault force had been spotted by radar at midnight and kept under close observation ever since. The searchlights, the guns and the fighters were all standing by, so that two minutes sufficed "to sweep everything out of the water".

But in fact something was still afloat not far from Malta—Giobbe's motor-boat and the two MAS. The fighters threw themselves on this new target. As dawn was breaking, the Italian boats were machine-gunned from deck-level. One MAS caught fire and the other was hit repeatedly. Moccagatta, Giobbe, Parodi, Falcomatà, Montanari, Costantini and Zocchi were all killed. The British lost one aircraft.

So ended the attack on Malta, the most daring and complex operation carried out by our Special Forces. It was brought to a tragic end by a combination of bad luck and unexpected difficulties; but there was, perhaps, no other operation which so well displayed the courage and patriotism of Italian seamen.

CHAPTER XXIV

## *OLTERRA'S* COMMANDER

*O*LTERRA was Visintini's masterpiece. The original idea of turning an old tub at Algeciras into a special instrument of war was not his alone; but it was he who transformed the battered tanker into a jumping-off base, entirely unsuspected by the British, for the assault forces which were to operate against Gibraltar.

He set up a workshop in the ship's hold and a sort of wet-dock from which to launch the "pigs"; he organised a continuous watch on shipping in the British port, and directed and inspired the men of the Special Force—*Ursa Major* as it was later called—which was to attack the British Mediterranean stronghold.

Visintini was quite at home at Gibraltar. He had been there on the night of 26th May 1941, and again the following September, in the submarine *Scirè* under the command of Borghese, who moved about in the Straits during the war as freely as if he were on manoeuvres off Spezia. Visintini's visits to Gibraltar, before he settled down on the salvaged tanker at La Linea, had, of course, taken place at night and had been confined to the waters of the harbour; he had not set foot on the quay or in the streets of the fortress. On the first occasion they had set out to attack merchant ships in the harbour, but, although Visintini reached the ship he was to mine, the attack was a failure. The second attempt was more successful, because they not only sank and damaged some ships, but Visintini and his number two got right into the inner basin, as Birindelli had done in the unfortunate expedition of October 1940.

Visintini penetrated the inner basin once more, in December 1942, but this time, as we shall see, it cost him his life, and in spite of many determined attempts no Italian ever got in again. I do not wish to detract in any way from the courage or the ability of the later frogmen who were among the most experienced in the Navy, but mention it in order to emphasize how difficult it was for them to pierce the triple line of nets, even when they and their torpedoes were launched from *Scirè* close by, below the mouth of the Guadarranque.

After his failure in May 1941 Visintini made his second and successful attempt on 20th September that year. Three pairs of frogmen were launched by *Scirè*, two of which attached their torpedoes to tankers in the main anchorage. The third pair, Visintini and Magro, made straight for the fleet anchorage. They outwitted the guard boats and the depth-charges exploding round them (a new departure, this), eluded the sentries and searchlights and got over the nets and steel cables barring the entrance. It was a terrible risk; but anchored inside were the battleship *Nelson*, the aircraft carrier *Ark Royal*, a couple of cruisers, many destroyers and some tankers—all targets well worth the risk.

Once inside, Visintini consulted the luminous dial of his wrist-watch. It was five past four; it had taken him nearly four hours to cover about three sea miles and penetrate the port defences. He surfaced at once to reconnoitre the possibilities left to him in the limited time available. The major targets, *Ark Royal* and *Nelson*, were moored too far down the bay, so he had to choose between the cruiser *Leander*, anchored near him, and a big tanker lying alongside the Detached Mole. He plumped for the tanker, in the hope that her considerable cargo of oil would catch fire when she blew up and damage *Leander*, *Ark Royal*, *Nelson* and other ships as well. This proved a false hope, for the oil did not catch fire, any more than it did in the tanker mined by Martellotto two months later at Alexandria. It would appear from this that the fuel oil used by the British was much less highly-refined than we had supposed.

Visintini and Magro, having left their little present of 600-lbs of explosive in the belly of the tanker *Derbydale*, succeeded in making their way out of the harbour and landed on the Spanish coast at 6.30 a.m. after six and a half hours in the water. *Derbydale* blew up at 8.45 a.m. at about the same time as the tankers *Durham* and *Fiona Shell* in the outer harbour, where they had been mined by the other two pairs of frogmen from *Scirè*. Precious oil tankers to the tune of thirty thousand tons were thus sunk or irreparably damaged without loss to the Italians. All the frogmen returned safely to Italy.

After two trips to Gibraltar and two arduous years with the assault forces, leading a life which necessitated the utmost physical fitness, Visintini might well have asked for leave. But he did not do so then, any more than he did at the time of his marriage to the woman he had loved for so long, or, in February 1941, when he heard that his airforce brother, Mario, had been killed in East Africa after shooting down seventeen enemy aircraft. On this occasion, his commanding officer had offered him an alternative posting, as he was now the sole support of his widowed mother; but Visintini replied that the death of his brother, posthumously awarded the Gold Cross, was an added inducement to him to carry out his own duty right to the end.

It was, in fact, after his brother's death that the two Gibraltar expeditions took place and it seems almost as if the figures of his brother and of his father, that great Istrian patriot, upheld him and inspired him to ever greater daring. In November 1941, he wrote to his fiancée: "I know that they can hear me and are proud of me, as I am of them, even to tears. Our family history is coming to an end, because everything has been given to Italy. . . . We talk and smile, secure in the knowledge that the Great Ones are guiding us."

He served with me in *Torelli* on an Atlantic patrol in September 1940, and I remember clearly his seriousness, his dedicated purpose, his professional skill and his indomitable spirit. Before joining *Torelli* he had asked to be transferred to the underwater assault forces. At Bordeaux, when we arrived there with the submarine, he received the news that his application had been granted; he left at once for Spezia and at the base on the Serchio he lived with Tesei, Toschi, de La Penne and Marceglia. With these four, later so distinguished, he completed his training on S.L.C.s.

After the second attack on Gibraltar, Visintini might well have sat back. But he was not satisfied. Perhaps he was still dreaming of those big British ships anchored at the far end of the bay just out of his reach. So, in the winter of 1942, he started an impressively realistic training of new frogmen and by the following summer he was in Spain getting *Olterra* ready.

Full details of the transformation of *Olterra* have already appeared in the works of Cappellini, Borghese and Spigai, and also in Italian and foreign newspapers and reviews. So I will not give a technical account here of how *Olterra* was fitted out or the frogmen and their torpedoes launched. What is, however, less well-known is Visintini's diary, in which he recorded all his thoughts throughout the war. In it we read, pencilled in his small, firm handwriting, a lively account of his day's work; his operational notes—observations on the defence of Gibraltar, the movements of ships in the harbour, the people he had met in the course of his work or whom he had seen near *Olterra*. Mixed up with this was everything he would have liked to say to Maria, his wife whom he had married a few days before leaving Italy, and whose love for him had grown to an almost mystical devotion.

I have seen few documents so full of poetry. It is a pity that those who put the exploits of our Special Forces on the screen, did not think to draw on it, when they wanted a contrast with the action-sequences, instead of introducing belly-dancers and slinky adventuresses.

But we must now come back to *Olterra*, which was very soon in operation. By the late summer of 1942, Visintini was able to put up to the 10th Flotilla his own plan for the employment of the pilots posted to or earmarked for the tanker. It was a simple plan, which can be summarised as follows:

(1) Nothing was to be done until a large warship entered Gibraltar, the waiting period being employed to make a minute study of the enemy's defensive measures;

(2) As soon as the big ships arrived, they were to be attacked at once by three "pigs."

It will be noted that Visintini did not even consider using *Olterra* to attack the cargo-boats berthed in the merchant-ship anchorage outside the boom, which was

199

also carefully patrolled. His aim was bolder and more ambitious.

You must remember that it was now well on in 1942. England had suffered losses at Suda Bay and in Alexandria; she had also seen a big tanker blow up in Gibraltar itself. Her defensive measures were therefore at a maximum. The boom-nets had been multiplied and an almost uninterrupted mine-barrage laid across the mouth of the harbour. But there are no obstacles for a daring man. Visintini had put up an audacious plan and, when it was approved, set about executing it with a careful attention to detail, which was remarkable in a young man of twenty-seven. He prepared his men and his weapons, studied the set of the currents and perfected his knowledge of the defences, observing the searchlights, gunboats, patrols and submarine mines. Then he sat down to wait for the British Navy.

He did not have to wait very long. On 6th December the battleships *Nelson* and *Renown* entered the harbour with the aircraft-carriers *Furious* and *Formidable* and a number of smaller ships. Activity round the boom was intensified. The little guard-boats bustled about; searchlights lit up the harbour almost continuously; and automatic mines went of every three minutes. Across the entrance to the naval basin, the explosions were almost continuous. Nevertheless, on the night of the 7th the men from *Olterra* came out from their base to attack the enemy. Visintini allocated the targets as follows: for himself and Magro, the battleship *Nelson*; for Cella and Leone, the aircraft-carrier *Furious*; for Manisco and Varini, the aircraft-carrier *Formidable*.

To reach their objectives they had to find a way into the naval basin, running the gauntlet of guard-boats, searchlights and patrols; break through the nets and get across the mined area. But, as Visintini wrote in his diary: "Nothing but death can stop us." He went into the attack without hesitation and, according to a British account, did in fact succeed in getting right into the naval basin.

This report says: "At 2.15 a.m. on 8th December three assault-craft carrying two men each tried to enter Gibraltar harbour. One was seen by a sentry, illuminated and then attacked and sunk by gunfire and depth-charges. The crew were picked up by a merchant ship. It is thought that they had been brought from Italy by the submarine *Ambra*. A second pair got into the naval basin, but were destroyed by depth-charges, while a third pair are thought to have died before reaching the basin."

It is not true, as we know, that the attackers had been launched from a submarine. (The mistake shows how well the secret of *Olterra* had been kept.) It is also partly untrue to say that the third pair died before reaching the harbour. In fact, though Leone disappeared, Cella was able to return to *Olterra*. On the other hand it is true that one pair—Visintini and Magro—succeeded in getting inside the naval basin. Having done so, they were killed in the mine-belt into which they had boldly plunged.

The bodies of Visintini and Magro came to the surface inside the harbour a few days later. They were buried at sea with full military honours; and a wreath was contributed by Lieuts. Crabbe and Bayley of the Gibraltar security-force.

# APPENDIX

## ITALIAN SUBMARINES IN THE ATLANTIC

| Submarine | C.O. who carried out the transfer | Remarks |
|---|---|---|
| FINZI | Dominici | Later under command of Giudice. Disarmed at Bordeaux at the Armistice. |
| TAZZOLI | Raccanelli | Under command of Fecia di Cossato, sank 100,000 tons of enemy shipping. Under command of Caito, disappeared without trace. |
| CALVI | Caridi | Under command of Longobardo was sunk by corvette *Lulworth* 14th July 1942. |
| TORELLI | Cocchia | Later commanded by Longobardo. Turned over, under command of Groppallo, to transport for Far East; was captured by the Germans at the Armistice. |
| MALASPINA | Leoni | Disappeared without trace while under the command of Prini. |
| BIANCHI | Giovannini | Later under command of Tosoni. Sunk by submarine *Severn* on 7th August 1941. |
| BARACCA | Bertarelli | Sunk by *Croome*, 8th September 1941, while under command of Viani. |
| FAA' DI BRUNO | Enrici | Sunk by destroyer *Havelock*, 8th November 1940. |
| CAPPELLINI | Todaro | First mission—to Ceuta—under Masa; after Todaro, passed to Ravedin and then to Auconi, under whom eventually turned over to Far East transport. Captured by the Germans at the Armistice. |
| VENIERO | Petroni | First passage, submerged, under command of Buonamici. Repatriated August '41 and sunk from the air south of the Balearics, under command of Zappetta. |
| MOCENIGO | Agostini | Repatriated August 1941. Sunk by aircraft at Cagliari 13th May 1943. |
| GLAUCO | Mellina | Under command of Baroni, was sunk by *Wishart* 27th June 1941. |

| Submarine | C.O. who carried out the transfer | Remarks |
|---|---|---|
| OTARIA | Vocaturo | Repatriated August 1941. |
| BRIN | Longanesi | Ditto. |
| TARANTINI | Iaschi | Sunk 15th December 1940 by submarine *Thunderbolt*. |
| GIULIANI | D'Elia | Turned over, under the command of Tei, to Far East transport. Captured at Singapore. |
| BAGNOLINI | Tosoni Pittoni | Disarmed at Bordeaux at the Armistice. |
| MARCONI | Chialamberto | Disappeared without trace. |
| DA VINCI | Calda | Later commanded by Gazzana who sank 60,000 tons of enemy shipping in one mission. Sank by English destroyers while returning to base 23rd May 1943. |
| EMO | Liannazza | Repatriated. Sunk 10th November 1942 by destroyer *Lord Nuffield* off Algiers. C.O. Franco. |
| MOROSINI | Criscuolo | Disappeared without trace 8th August 1942. C.O. D'Alessendro. |
| NANI | Polizzi | Sunk 7th January 1941 by the corvette *Anemone*. |
| MARCELLO | Teppati | Sunk by aircraft 6th Feb. 1941. |
| BARBARIGO | Chiglieri | Later commanded by Grossi. Sunk without trace while under command of De Julio. |
| DANDOLO | Boris | Repatriated in summer of 1941. |
| ARGO | Crepas | Repatriated and scuppered at the Armistice. |
| VELELLA | Terra | Repatriated. Sunk 7th Sept. 1943 by the submarine *Shakespeare*. |
| ARCHIMEDE | Spagone | Arrived from Massaua. Sunk from the air 15th April 1943 on the coast of Brazil. C.O. Saccardo. |
| FERRARIS | Piomarta | Arrived from Massaua. Sunk after surface battle with destroyer *Lamerton* 25th October 1941. |
| GUGLIEL-MOTTI | Salvatori | Repatriated from Massaua. Sunk by submarine *Unbeaten* 17th March 1942. C.O. Tamburni. |
| PERLA | Nappi | Repatriated from Massaua. Lost 9th July 1942 off the Syrian coast. C.O. Ventura. |
| CAGNI | Liannazza | Completed profitable mission under Roselli. Repatriated after the Armistice through Suez. |

# RAMSAY AT WAR

*The Fighting Life of Admiral Sir Bertram Ramsay*
K.C.B., K.B.E., M.V.O.

## *by*

## David Woodward
Author of *The Tirpitz*

Admiral Ramsay was responsible for the planning and execution of all the great amphibious operations in European and North African waters from Dunkirk to D-Day. As Vice-Admiral at Dover he organized the evacuation from Dunkirk, the defence of South-East England against threatened invasion, and the regular sailing of coast-wise convoys past the German batteries and E-boats. Later he was appointed to make the naval plans for the Second Front. Then he planned and helped carry out the landings in North Africa, Sicily and Italy.

Finally he was made Allied Naval Commander-in-Chief for the D-Day landings in France and the operations which cleared the mouth of the river Scheldt and made possible the build-up for the final advance into Germany. This, however, he did not live to see for he was killed in an air crash on January 2nd, 1945, and is buried in France, the country he did so much to free.

The story of Admiral Ramsay is written with facilities granted by the Admiralty and from the personal narratives of those who took part in the operations for which he was responsible. It is a thrilling record of a great man of action.

*Demy*        *Illustrated*        18s. *net*

# CONVOY COMMODORE

## *by*

## Rear-Admiral Sir Kenelm Creighton

K.B.E., M.V.O.

On September 4th, 1939, Admiral Creighton, who had retired from the Navy five years earlier, reported again to the Admiralty for service as a Commodore of Ocean Convoys. In the following three years he conducted 24 convoys to various parts of the world.

The greater part of this time was spent on the North Atlantic route with its violent storms and the continual menace of U-boat attack. But there were other destinations, such as Suez via the Cape of Good Hope, and Casablanca—where the convoy sailed to repatriate 15,000 French troops after the fall of France, and found itself under arrest. In 1941 Admiral Creighton narrowly escaped with his life when the ship he was in was sunk by a U-boat near Gibraltar. Another ship in which he was travelling as a passenger, accompanied by his wife, was torpedoed and sunk by German aircraft.

Besides a wealth of personal experiences, Admiral Creighton gives us a broader picture of the work done by convoys throughout the last war. From his senior position, and with an intimate knowledge of the subject, he is able to convey graphically the true nature of this dangerous and vital task.

*Demy*                     *Illustrated*                     18s. *net*

# THROUGH THE WATERS

*Life Aboard a Fighting Cruiser*

*by*

## Robert Hughes

The author was an officer on *Scylla* during most of her active career; his book is a personal account of his experiences on board. *Scylla* was an efficient fighting cruiser but, under the strict, kindly rule of Captain MacIntyre, she was also something like a home.

Her first task was to act as flagship to the famous P.Q.18. Russian convoy. They fought their way through enemy controlled waters, keeping up a non-stop battle that lasted for days and cost them thirteen ships, but the remainder reached Murmansk. *Scylla* had come through her first ordeal with flying colours and was cheered in by the fleet on her return to Scapa.

*Scylla* next took part in the landings in North Africa and escorted supply and transport ships in the Mediterranean, protecting them from the desperate attacks of U-boats. It was *Scylla* who took on the survivors of the ill-fated *Ibis*, and *Scylla* who intercepted the blockade runner *Rhakotis,* thus dealing the final blow against the German surface raiders.

Once again *Scylla* departed on a Russian convoy; this time the enemies were the paralysing Arctic cold and the heavy seas; two transports broke in half in the mountainous waves.

*Scylla* now returned to patrolling in the Bay of Biscay and convoys round Cape St. Vincent. The air attacks were no longer venomously pressed home; the enemy were losing heart. And so on to the Salerno landings and onto the offensive; the glider bomb put in its appearance with devastating effect.

Eighteen months of strenuous fighting and several near misses then took their effect and *Scylla* had to return home for a refit. She was only to reappear once more, at the Normandy landings; she hit a mine and barely made harbour.

Robert Hughes had a great affection for *Scylla* and her crew—most of them had joined together on commissioning—and through the dramatic story of a fighting cruiser's vicissitudes shine the enduring values of the friendship and bravery of sailors at war.

*Demy*  *Illustrated*  18s. net

# STAND BY FOR ACTION

*A Sailor's Story*

*by*

## Commander William Donald

D.S.C. & Bar

At the outbreak of the war the author was a young naval officer serving as First Lieutenant of a sloop. His first mission was to Norway, and he gives a vivid account of the suspense and nervous strain of operating in the narrow waters of a twisting fjord under heavy air attack. He had his first escape when his ship got a direct hit from a bomb which did not explode.

His next task—in command first of a corvette and then of a destroyer—was escorting East Coast convoys, and his experiences reflect the excitement and danger of this work against the menaces of E-boats, enemy aircraft and mines. After being given the command of a new destroyer he takes part in the landing at Anzio and in further naval actions in the Mediterranean.

The Normandy landing was the next great phase of the war in which Commander Donald participated, and when the war in Europe had ended he continued his active career in the Far East where his narrative ends with the relief of Hong Kong and the liberation of British P.o.W.s.

Commander Donald's record of varied and almost incessant action ranks among the most thrilling personal stories of the war at sea.

*Demy*                    *Illustrated*                    18s. *net*